HOW DATA MINING THREATENS
STUDENT PRIVACY

JOINT HEARING

BEFORE THE

SUBCOMMITTEE ON CYBERSECURITY,
INFRASTRUCTURE PROTECTION,
AND SECURITY TECHNOLOGIES

OF THE

COMMITTEE ON HOMELAND SECURITY
HOUSE OF REPRESENTATIVES
Serial No. 113–76

AND THE

SUBCOMMITTEE ON EARLY CHILDHOOD,
ELEMENTARY, AND SECONDARY EDUCATION

OF THE

COMMITTEE ON EDUCATION
AND THE WORKFORCE
HOUSE OF REPRESENTATIVES
Serial No. 113–61

ONE HUNDRED THIRTEENTH CONGRESS

SECOND SESSION

JUNE 25, 2014

Printed for the use of the Committee on Homeland Security and the
Committee on Education and the Workforce

Available via the World Wide Web: http://www.gpo.gov/fdsys/

U.S. GOVERNMENT PRINTING OFFICE

91–448 PDF   WASHINGTON : 2015

For sale by the Superintendent of Documents, U.S. Government Printing Office
Internet: bookstore.gpo.gov Phone: toll free (866) 512–1800; DC area (202) 512–1800
Fax: (202) 512–2250 Mail: Stop SSOP, Washington, DC 20402–0001

COMMITTEE ON HOMELAND SECURITY

MICHAEL T. McCAUL, Texas, *Chairman*

LAMAR SMITH, Texas
PETER T. KING, New York
MIKE ROGERS, Alabama
PAUL C. BROUN, Georgia
CANDICE S. MILLER, Michigan, *Vice Chair*
PATRICK MEEHAN, Pennsylvania
JEFF DUNCAN, South Carolina
TOM MARINO, Pennsylvania
JASON CHAFFETZ, Utah
STEVEN M. PALAZZO, Mississippi
LOU BARLETTA, Pennsylvania
RICHARD HUDSON, North Carolina
STEVE DAINES, Montana
SUSAN W. BROOKS, Indiana
SCOTT PERRY, Pennsylvania
MARK SANFORD, South Carolina
VACANCY

BENNIE G. THOMPSON, Mississippi
LORETTA SANCHEZ, California
SHEILA JACKSON LEE, Texas
YVETTE D. CLARKE, New York
BRIAN HIGGINS, New York
CEDRIC L. RICHMOND, Louisiana
WILLIAM R. KEATING, Massachusetts
RON BARBER, Arizona
DONDALD M. PAYNE, JR., New Jersey
BETO O'ROURKE, Texas
FILEMON VELA, Texas
ERIC SWALWELL, California
VACANCY
VACANCY

BRENDAN P. SHIELDS, *Staff Director*
JOAN O'HARA, *Acting Chief Counsel*
MICHAEL S. TWINCHEK, *Chief Clerk*
I. LANIER AVANT, *Minority Staff Director*

———

SUBCOMMITTEE ON CYBERSECURITY, INFRASTRUCTURE PROTECTION, AND SECURITY TECHNOLOGIES

PATRICK MEEHAN, Pennsylvania, *Chairman*

MIKE ROGERS, Alabama
TOM MARINO, Pennsylvania
JASON CHAFFETZ, Utah
STEVE DAINES, Montana
SCOTT PERRY, Pennsylvania, *Vice Chair*
MICHAEL T. McCAUL, Texas *(ex officio)*

YVETTE D. CLARKE, New York
WILLIAM R. KEATING, Massachusetts
FILEMON VELA, Texas
VACANCY
BENNIE G. THOMPSON, Mississippi *(ex officio)*

ALEX MANNING, *Subcommittee Staff Director*
DENNIS TERRY, *Subcommittee Clerk*

COMMITTEE ON EDUCATION AND THE WORKFORCE

JOHN KLINE, Minnesota, *Chairman*

THOMAS E. PETRI, Wisconsin
HOWARD P. "BUCK" MCKEON, California
JOE WILSON, South Carolina
VIRGINIA FOXX, North Carolina
TOM PRICE, Georgia
KENNY MARCHANT, Texas
DUNCAN HUNTER, California
DAVID P. ROE, Tennessee
GLENN THOMPSON, Pennsylvania
TIM WALBERG, Michigan
MATT SALMON, Arizona
BRETT GUTHRIE, Kentucky
SCOTT DESJARLAIS, Tennessee
TODD ROKITA, Indiana
LARRY BUCSHON, Indiana
LOU BARLETTA, Pennsylvania
JOSEPH J. HECK, Nevada
MIKE KELLY, Pennsylvania
SUSAN W. BROOKS, Indiana
RICHARD HUDSON, North Carolina
LUKE MESSER, Indiana
BRADLEY BYRNE, Alabama

GEORGE MILLER, California,
  Senior Democratic Member
ROBERT C. "BOBBY" SCOTT, Virginia
RUBÉN HINOJOSA, Texas
CAROLYN MCCARTHY, New York
JOHN F. TIERNEY, Massachusetts
RUSH HOLT, New Jersey
SUSAN A. DAVIS, California
RAÚL M. GRIJALVA, Arizona
TIMOTHY H. BISHOP, New York
DAVID LOEBSACK, Iowa
JOE COURTNEY, Connecticut
MARCIA L. FUDGE, Ohio
JARED POLIS, Colorado
GREGORIO KILILI CAMACHO SABLAN,
  Northern Mariana Islands
FREDERICA S. WILSON, Florida
SUZANNE BONAMICI, Oregon
MARK POCAN, Wisconsin
MARK TAKANO, California

JULIANE SULLIVAN, *Staff Director*
MEGAN O'REILLY, *Minority Staff Director*

———

SUBCOMMITTEE ON EARLY CHILDHOOD, ELEMENTARY, AND SECONDARY EDUCATION

TODD ROKITA, Indiana, *Chairman*

JOHN KLINE, Minnesota
THOMAS E. PETRI, Wisconsin
VIRGINIA FOXX, North Carolina
KENNY MARCHANT, Texas
DUNCAN HUNTER, California
DAVID P. ROE, Tennessee
GLENN THOMPSON, Pennsylvania
SUSAN W. BROOKS, Indiana
BRADLEY BYRNE, Alabama

DAVID LOEBSACK, Iowa,
  Ranking Minority Member
ROBERT C. "BOBBY" SCOTT, Virginia
CAROLYN MCCARTHY, New York
SUSAN A. DAVIS, California
RAÚL M. GRIJALVA, Arizona
MARCIA L. FUDGE, Ohio
JARED POLIS, Colorado
GREGORIO KILILI CAMACHO SABLAN,
  Northern Mariana Islands

CONTENTS

FOR THE RECORD

HOW DATA MINING THREATENS STUDENT PRIVACY

————

Wednesday, June 25, 2014

U.S. HOUSE OF REPRESENTATIVES,
COMMITTEE ON HOMELAND SECURITY,
SUBCOMMITTEE ON CYBERSECURITY,
INFRASTRUCTURE PROTECTION, AND
SECURITY TECHNOLOGIES, AND
U.S. HOUSE OF REPRESENTATIVES,
COMMITTEE ON EDUCATION AND THE WORKFORCE,
SUBCOMMITTEE ON THE EARLY CHILDHOOD,
ELEMENTARY, AND SECONDARY EDUCATION,
Washington, DC.

The subcommittees met, pursuant to call, at 11:02 a.m., in Room 311, Cannon House Office Building, Hon. Patrick Meehan [Chairman of the Cybersecurity, Infrastructure Protection, and Security Technologies subcommittee] presiding.

Present from Subcommittee on Cybersecurity, Infrastructure Protection, and Security Technologies: Representatives Meehan, Rogers, Clarke, and Vela.

Present from Subcommittee on Early Childhood, Elementary, and Secondary Education: Representatives Rokita, Roe, Brooks, and Loebsack.

Also present: Representative Bonamici.

Mr. MEEHAN. The Subcommittee on Cybersecurity, Infrastructure Protection, and Security Technologies of the Committee on Homeland Security and the Subcommittee on Early Childhood, Elementary, and Secondary Education of the Committee on Education and the Workforce will now come to order. The subcommittees are jointly meeting today to examine data collection and privacy concerns in education.

I will recognize myself for an opening statement. I would like to thank Ranking Member Clarke, as well as Chairman Rokita and Ranking Member Loebsack from the Education and the Workforce Subcommittee on Early Childhood, Elementary, and Secondary Education, for coming together with us today to hold this joint hearing on what is a very important issue, which is the privacy and security of our students' Personally Identifiable Information. We call it PII. Today marks the first joint hearing between these two committees, and I am looking forward to working with Chairman Rokita and Ranking Members Clarke and Loebsack on this issue.

In recent years, the number of school districts using educational software and cloud services has just exponentially increased.

(1)

Today, nearly 95 percent of school districts are using these services. These services can provide numerous advantages to school administrators and educators, including individualized learning, State examination assessments and administrative functions such as attendance records. While these services can be helpful to our students' development, it is vitally important that we understand the privacy and security concerns of sharing such sensitive information.

A report by the Fordham Law School found that cloud services used by school districts are poorly understood and have a lack of transparency, finding 20 percent of school districts do not have proper policies in place for the use of these services. Fewer than 7 percent restrict the sale of student information by vendors. Let me repeat that line: Fewer than 7 percent restrict the sale of student information by vendors. Security of student information must be paramount. As this subcommittee has examined in recent hearings, cyber criminals have become more sophisticated in their tactics and techniques, evidenced by the increasing number of cyber breaches at universities, schools, and retailers. The more convenienced our lives become with on-line services the greater risk these criminals can exploit it.

Over the past year, three major universities and one school district became victims of cyber breaches affecting hundreds of thousands of students' personally identifiable information. But it is not just the identifiable information. It is also information about the students and their performance itself. Much like health records, a lot of the things that is being able to be tracked includes the mental processes of students as they are working through equations. There has to be an appropriate form of protection of that, an appropriate form of parental consent, before that kind of information is utilized.

Greater transparency is needed on behalf of the school districts and the vendors with which they contract. Parents enrolling their children in school should have a clear understanding of what information is collected, stored, and shared. The Family Educational Rights and Privacy Act, which we call FERPA, is the Federal law that governs the privacy of student records. FERPA establishes when, and what type, of information school districts can share with private vendors. However, there are concerns that because FERPA was enacted in 1974, long before the advent of these technologies, it doesn't reflect the current reality in the classroom and changes in how data is collected and shared.

I think we will also hear testimony about gaps that exist in the laws that oversee the protection of student information. Today's hearing will seek to examine the sharing of student information with educational software and cloud service vendors, and the laws and guidelines that govern them. The subcommittees will hear testimony from a distinguished panel, including representatives from the Fordham Law School, Software and Information Industry Association, the Idaho State Department of Education, and the Alliance for Excellent Education.

Transparency on behalf of the school districts and the educational companies is vitally important. Parents should have a clear understanding of what schools are sharing and what rights they have. I appreciate the opportunity to work with my colleagues in Education and the Workforce to examine this important issue.

[The statement of Chairman Meehan follows:]

STATEMENT OF CHAIRMAN PATRICK MEEHAN

JUNE 25, 2014

I would like to thank Ranking Member Clarke as well as Chairman Rokita and Ranking Member Loebsack from the Education and the Workforce Subcommittee on Early Childhood, Elementary, and Secondary Education for corning together with us to hold this joint hearing on a very important issue, the privacy and security of our students' Personally Identifiable Information (PII). Today marks the first joint hearing between these two committees, and I'm looking forward to working with Chairman Rokita and Ranking Member Loebsack on this issue.

In recent years the number of school districts using educational software and cloud services has greatly increased; today nearly 95% of school districts are using these services. These services can provide numerous advantages to school administrations and educators including individualized learning, State examination assessments, and administrative functions such as attendance records. While these services can be helpful to our student's development, it is vitally important that we understand the privacy and security concerns of sharing such sensitive information. A report by the Fordham Law School found that cloud services used by school districts are poorly understood and have a lack of transparency, finding 20% of school districts do not have proper policies in place for the use of these services and fewer than 7% restrict the sale of student information by vendors.

Security of student information must be paramount, as this subcommittee has examined in recent hearings cyber criminals have become more sophisticated in their tactics and techniques, evidenced by the increasing number of cyber breaches at universities, schools, and retailers. The more interconnected our lives become with online services the greater the risk these criminals can exploit it. Over the past year three major universities and one school district have become victims of cyber breaches affecting hundreds of thousands of students' Personally Identifiable Information.

Greater transparency is needed on behalf of the school districts and the vendors with which they contract. Parents enrolling their children in school should have a clear understanding of what information is collected, stored, and shared. The Family Educational Rights and Privacy Act (FERPA) is the Federal law that governs the privacy of student records. FERPA establishes when and what type of information school districts can share with private vendors. However, there are concerns that because FERPA was enacted in 1974, long before the advent of these technologies, it does not reflect the current reality in the classroom and the changes in how data is collected and shared.

Today's hearing will seek to examine the sharing of student information with educational software and cloud service vendors and the laws and guidelines that govern them. The subcommittees will hear testimony from a distinguished panel including representatives from the Fordham Law School, Software and Information Industry Association, Idaho State Department of Education, and the Alliance for Excellent Education. Transparency on behalf of the school districts and the educational companies is vitally important; parents should have a clear understanding of what schools are sharing and what rights they have. I appreciate the opportunity to work with my colleagues at Education and the Workforce to examine this important issue.

Mr. MEEHAN. The Chairman now recognizes the Ranking Member of the subcommittee, the gentlelady from New York, for any statements she may have.

Ms. CLARKE. Thank you, Mr. Chairman. I want to thank you for holding today's hearing. I want to welcome our colleagues from the Education and the Workforce Committee, especially Ranking Member Loebsack and his fellow Members from the Early Childhood, Elementary, and Secondary Education Subcommittee.

Today's hearing reminds me of the work we have done on this subcommittee in developing authorities for the Department of Homeland Security to create a robust cyber workforce. In developing my bill, Cybersecurity Boots on the Ground, we thought carefully about how we must learn to improve the readiness and capacity of DHS' cybersecurity current workforce. But more importantly, how to engineer systems and devices that earn parents, schools, and policymakers' trust and confidence to train students for future careers. Our goal was to encourage innovation in education to help create cyber-capable citizens and help sustain a cyber-capable workforce.

Today's hearing is specifically about the use of technology in learning that could open up countless opportunities for students from the personalization of learning to the concept of learning any time, anywhere. From visiting the schools in my district, I have seen how advanced technology is being rapidly deployed in all grades and can offer benefits that support a number of distinct functions, from data analytics to student reporting requirements to basic productivity, functions such as e-mail, data storage, and document editing. Advances in information technology have led to many new ways to collect data, analyze and use data, in ever-expanding volumes.

Big data holds tremendous potential to benefit society and contribute to economic growth. Researchers have told us that it will soon be possible to create and maintain longitudinal data about the abilities and learning styles of millions of students. Early adopters of these technologies have demonstrated their potential to transform and advance educational tools. But these same technologies also called attention to serious policy questions. In particular, the information-sharing web hosting and telecommunication innovations that have enabled these new educational technologies raise questions about how best to protect student privacy and about the security of student information.

In this committee's work on cybersecurity legislation, we have seen that rapidly-developing technology like data mining often outpaces the capacities and legal requirements that institutions and businesses need to manage and make use of big data and information sharing.

However, data mining has emerged as one of the few—the key features of many Homeland Security programs involving the use of sophisticated data analysis tools to discover previously-unknown valid patterns and relationships and learning enlarged data sets. In the context of homeland security, data mining is viewed as an essential means to identify terrorists and criminal activities, such as money transfers and communications screens and to identify and track terrorists themselves through travel and immigration records.

However, the concept of data mining in education has witnessed dramatic world-wide growth both in academia and in the business sector as a process that can provide useful data necessary for decision making in institutions and for the development of educational tools. While States and local communities are the core of our education systems, much of the software that supports on-line learning tools, on-line courses, and school system productivity tools is provided by for-profit firms. This raises complicated questions about who owns the data streams coming off on-line education platforms and how they are used.

Applying priority safeguards to educational records can create unique tasks. Today, we will hear how the use of school-based student data has gained more attention in recent months and how it has seen increased scrutiny by parents and advocates and resulted in new State and local laws.

I know that my colleagues on the Education and the Workforce Committee, Mr. Polis and others, are working with a variety of stakeholders to find the right balance for educational settings. I also know that the technology industry is already engaged, working on best practices and policies, along with a number of expert and academic organizations, to move these discussions along.

I look forward to the testimony of our distinguished panelists today, Mr. Chairman, and I yield back.

[The statement of Ranking Member Clarke follows:]

STATEMENT OF RANKING MEMBER YVETTE D. CLARKE

JUNE 25, 2014

Today's hearing reminds me of the work we have done on this subcommittee in developing authorities for the Department of Homeland Security to create a robust cyber workforce. In developing my bill, "Cybersecurity Boots on the Ground", we thought carefully about how we must learn to improve the readiness and capacity of DHS's cybersecurity current workforce, but more importantly, how to engineer systems and devices that earn parents, schools, and policy maker's trust and confidence, to train students for future careers. Our goal was to encourage innovation in education to help create "cyber-capable" citizens, and help sustain a "cyber-capable" workforce.

Today's hearing is specifically about the use of technology in learning that could open up countless opportunities for students, from the "personalization of learning", to the concept of "learning anytime and anywhere". From visiting the schools in my district, I have seen how advanced technology is being rapidly deployed in all grades, and can offer benefits that support a number of distinct functions, from data analytics, to student reporting requirements, to basic productivity functions such as email, data storage, and document editing.

Advances in information technology have led to many new ways to collect data, analyze, and use data in ever-expanding volumes. Big data holds tremendous potential to benefit society and contribute to economic growth. Researchers have told us that it will soon be possible to create and maintain longitudinal data about the abilities and learning styles of millions of students. Early adopters of these technologies have demonstrated their potential to transform and advance educational tools, but these same technologies have also called attention to serious policy questions. In particular, the information sharing, web-hosting, and telecommunication innovations that have enabled these new education technologies raise questions about how best to protect student privacy, and about the security of student information.

In this committee's work on cybersecurity legislation, we have seen that rapidly-developing technology, like data mining, often outpaces the capacities and legal requirements that institutions and businesses need to manage and make use of "big data" and information sharing. However, data mining has emerged as one of the key features of many homeland security programs, involving the use of sophisticated data analysis tools to discover previously unknown, valid patterns and relationships in large data sets. In the context of homeland security, data mining is viewed as an essential means to identify terrorist and criminal activities, such as money transfers and communications sources, and to identify and track terrorists themselves, through travel and immigration records.

However, the concept of data mining in education has witnessed dramatic worldwide growth, both in academia and in the business sector, as a process that can provide useful data necessary for decision making in institutions, and for the development of educational tools. While States and local communities are the core of our education systems, much of the software that supports on-line learning tools, on-line courses, and school system productivity tools, is provided by for-profit firms.

This raises complicated questions about who owns the data streams coming off on-line education platforms and how they are used. Applying privacy safeguards to educational records can create unique tasks. Today, we will hear how the use of school-based student data has gained more attention in recent months, and how it has seen increased scrutiny by parents and advocates, and resulted in new State and local laws.

I know that my colleagues on the Education and the Workforce Committee, Mr. Polis and others, are working with a variety of stakeholders to find the right balance for educational settings, and I also know that the technology industry is already engaged—working on best practices and policies, along with a number of expert and academic organizations to move these discussions along.

Mr. MEEHAN. I want to thank the Ranking Member, and I also want to express my deep appreciation to my colleague—my good friend and colleague, the gentleman from Indiana. This is one of those opportunities where we have the occasion in which our work overlaps. We had a shared interest, and I was very grateful for not only his agreement, but encouragement, to find a way in which we could jointly explore this so that we may learn a great deal and perhaps share in the resolution of the matter. So I am very grateful for your participation.

The Chairman now recognizes the Chairman of the Subcommittee on Early Childhood, Elementary, and Secondary Education, the gentleman from Indiana, Mr. Rokita, for any statement he may have.

Mr. ROKITA. Thank you, Chairman Meehan. Good morning and welcome. Let me begin by thanking you, Chairman, for approaching me and my committee Members about the idea for this morning's hearing. I am pleased that our two subcommittee teams came together for this important and relatively new issue. So again, thank you for your leadership. Collaboration across committees is very important, and I hope not only these two committees, but others, are able to do more of it.

As we draw from the knowledge and expertise of our House colleagues, I believe we become more effective policymakers. So I look forward, No. 1, from hearing from our witnesses and having an informative discussion.

We are dealing with an issue today that is both critically important and exceptionally complex. First, why is it so important? As we fight for all Americans looking to build better lives for themselves and their families, we know that a cornerstone of that is a quality education. It is the route of a better life. With very few exceptions, a worker will not succeed in the workforce if they failed as a student in the classroom. A strong education system is essential to a strong and exceptional America. That is why we should engage innovative solutions to raise achievement, and embrace new technologies that allow us to teach children in more effective ways.

We often see how acquiring data on student performance can revolutionize student learning. For starters, data can provide an early warning to teachers, alerting them to students who are falling behind and need that extra help. It can also awaken parents to the challenges their child is facing so they can step in with additional support at home. Additionally, data on student achievement can equip local communities with the information needed to hold their schools accountable as well as enable schools to share information on what is working in their classrooms. Sometimes even more importantly, what is not working.

So on to the next question: Why is this so complex? Well, I think we have learned by now that modern technology is anything but a simple concept. The science and ingenuity behind each new smartphone app, computer, or piece of software is tough to comprehend. Yet, these products have become an integral part of our everyday lives. Even though we surely got along before them, still it is hard to imagine what our daily lives would be like if we never heard the names such as Google, Apple, Microsoft, Facebook, and Amazon. With each new technology comes risk and responsibility.

That is certainly the case when it comes to the technology we bring into our schools and the data we collect on our students. Protecting student privacy is a shared responsibility. Parents have to be informed and engaged about what technologies and practices are used in their schools and what data is actually collected on their children, who has access to that data, and the safeguards in place to protect our children's privacy. What is the role of the local school board, local school leaders, and staff? Should State and local education leaders have to ensure they are limiting the data collected to only information truly needed to improve classroom instruction?

Who gets to define what "truly needed" means? Should access to student data be limited to only individuals who are working with schools to improve classroom instruction? Should there be strict security protocols in place, while ensuring parents are fully informed about the data use policies of the particular school or district? Then there are the technology providers, who I expect would agree, have an equally important role in protecting student privacy and securing student data to which they have access. These companies must remain vigilant and remember that students are in the classroom first and foremost to learn.

Finally, there is also a role for Federal policymakers that is Constitutionally-based. For example, for 40 years the Family Educational Rights and Privacy Act that Chairman Meehan mentioned has been in place to protect the privacy of student education records. I look forward to discussing with our witnesses today whether that law is up to the challenges that we face today, or whether changes need to be made so that the law better reflects the realities of modern technology, also as Chairman Meehan alluded to. Or is it simply a matter of all the stakeholders self-policing?

I am fighting for all people so that they can build better lives for themselves and their families. Strengthening education is a goal we all share, and one the Education and the Workforce Committee has spent a great deal of time working on. As I noted earlier, the gathering and sharing of student data can improve achievement, but let's make sure we are doing it in a way that doesn't have unintended consequences like losing student privacy.

Chairman Meehan, again thank you for your leadership and your help with this joint hearing.

[The statement of Chairman Rokita follows:]

STATEMENT OF CHAIRMAN TODD ROKITA

JUNE 25, 2014

Let me begin by thanking Chairman Meehan for hosting today's joint subcommittee hearing. Promoting collaboration across committees is important. As we draw from the knowledge and expertise of our House colleagues, I believe we become more effective policymakers. I look forward to hearing from our witnesses and to an informative discussion.

We are dealing with an issue today that is both critically important and exceptionally complex.

Why is it so important? As we fight for all Americans looking to build better lives for themselves and their families, we know that a quality education is at the root of that better life. With very few exceptions, a worker will not succeed in the workforce if they failed as a student in the classroom. A strong education system is essential to a strong America. That is why we should encourage innovative solutions to raise achievement and embrace new technologies that allow us to teach children in more effective ways.

We all can see how acquiring data on student performance can revolutionize student learning. For starters, data can provide an early warning to teachers, alerting them to students who are falling behind and need extra help. It can also awaken parents to the challenges their child is facing so they can step in with additional support at home. Additionally, data on student achievement can equip local communities with the information needed to hold their schools accountable, as well as enable schools to share information on what's working in their classrooms and what's not.

Why is it so complex? Well, I think we've learned by now that modern technology is anything but a simple concept. The science and ingenuity behind each new smart phone, app, computer, or piece of software is tough to comprehend, yet these products have become an integral part of our everyday lives. It's hard to imagine what life would be like if we never heard of names such as Apple, Microsoft, Google, and Amazon.

With each new technology comes risk and responsibility. That is certainly the case when it comes to the technology we bring into our schools and the data we collect on our students. Protecting student privacy is a shared responsibility.

Parents have to be informed and engaged about what technologies and practices are used in their schools, what data is actually collected on their children, who has access to that data, and the safeguards in place to protect their child's privacy.

State and local education leaders have to ensure they are limiting the data collected to only information truly needed to improve classroom instruction. That means they must limit access to student data to only individuals who are working with the schools to improve classroom instruction. They must also ensure there are strict security protocols in place while ensuring parents are fully informed about the data use policies of the school and district.

And then there are the technology providers, who have an equally important role in protecting student privacy and securing student data to which they have access. These companies must remain vigilant and remember that students are in the classroom first and foremost to learn. Data and student information should be placed in the hands of educators so they can leverage those resources to further student achievement.

Finally, there is also a role for Federal policymakers as well. We should oppose any information sharing or data mining on students intended to serve interests outside of the classroom. For 40 years the *Family Educational Rights and Privacy Act* has been in place to protect the privacy of student education records. I look forward to discussing with our witnesses today whether that law is up to the challenges we face today, or whether changes need to be made so that the law reflects the realities of modern technology.

Mr. MEEHAN. Let me thank Chairman Rokita. I would like to also express my deep appreciation to the Ranking Member, the gentleman from Iowa from the subcommittee, Mr. Loebsack.

You are recognized for any statement you may have.

Mr. LOEBSACK. Thank you, Chairman Meehan. It is great to be here with you and with Chairman Rokita and Ranking Member Clarke, as well. I do thank you for holding today's hearing, and I thank our witnesses for being here, as well.

More than ever before, technology plays an essential role in educating our children. I think we can all agree to that. Technology-based educational tools and platforms offer important new capabilities for students and teachers at both the K–12 and university levels. The increasing number of educational iPad and iPhone apps, on-line study tools and engagement programs illustrate the growing abundance of tech resources that are being used to meet students' individual learning needs. These educational tools generate tremendous amounts of data that are instrumental in improving a student's learning experience.

Data allow teachers to quickly identify and address gaps in student understanding before they fall behind. By making data available to parents, they can track their child's progress and participate more fully in their education. Beyond addressing the needs of individual students, data aids schools and their institutional and administrative functions. School and district leaders rely on data to drive improvement and decision making around curriculum, technology infrastructure, and staffing. The availability of new types of data also improves researchers' ability to learn about learning.

Data from a student's experience, and technology-based learning platforms, can be precisely tracked, opening the door to more accurately understanding how students move through a curriculum, and at greater scale than traditional education research is able to achieve. As data systems become more integrated into the learning and teaching process, we are seeing the impact that they can have on students, teachers, administrators, and policy makers. These systems enable teachers, schools, and districts to make more informed decisions to enhance student learning.

Meanwhile, a growing number of on-line educational services have the ability to enhance learning within the classroom and extend it beyond the school day. Edmodo, for example, which is used by more than 20 million teachers and students world-wide, allows teachers to set up virtual classrooms and then post homework assignments and other content to extend lessons. Khan Academy has more than 5,000 instructional videos and assessments which allow students of all ages to learn at their own pace in subject areas ranging from pre-algebra to differential equations, from art history to computer science.

With this explosion in on-line resources, there is a large amount of new data being generated by children using these services which do raise valid privacy concerns. The privacy of student education records, as we know, is protected under FERPA, the Family Educational Rights and Privacy Act. When those student education records are hosted or analyzed by private companies that are helping districts build data systems to drive improvement, those same FERPA protections still apply, and we have to keep that in mind. However, when students use on-line services like Khan Academy in school or at home, or when teachers use grade and behavior-tracking software on their iPads, all of that data are not necessarily covered by FERPA.

In those direct interactions between students and software companies, data are being collected to build user profiles, individualize the learning experience, and track progress. But in the cases where FERPA does not apply, it is not always clear what protections exist to guarantee the privacy of those data and ensure companies are not using them to target advertisements at children, for example. This committee will hear important testimony today about the value that these tailored technological resources provide the students themselves, and the importance of ensuring access to data for teachers and researchers to improve education.

We will also hear about the need for consistent privacy policies, and current efforts to generate the security and privacy of student data. As we examine the privacy concerns prompted by the rapidly-growing education technology sector and the information it collects, it is clear that we must strive to find a proper balance between privacy and innovation. We must ensure that companies involved in collecting and analyzing student data are not exploiting students' private information for marketing purposes or financial gain. Data are an invaluable tool. Data empower teachers, guide individualized learning, and inform policy.

As we consider where improvements are needed in privacy regulations, we must be sure that we do not compromise the value of student data. I look forward to hearing from the witnesses today.

Thank you, again, Chairman Meehan and Chairman Rokita and Ranking Member Clarke for this hearing. Thank you.

[The statement of Mr. Loebsack follows:]

STATEMENT OF HON. DAVID LOEBSACK

JUNE 25, 2014

Good morning, Chairman Rokita, Chairman Meehan, and Ranking Member Clarke. I'd like to thank you for holding today's hearing and thank our witnesses for being here.

More than ever before, technology plays an essential role in educating our children. Technology-based educational tools and platforms offer important new capabilities for students and teachers at both the K–12 and university levels.

The increasing number of educational iPad and iPhone apps, on-line study tools, and engagement programs illustrate the growing abundance of tech resources that are being used to meet students' individual learning needs.

These educational tools generate tremendous amounts of data that are instrumental in improving a student's learning experience. Data allows teachers to quickly identify and address gaps in student understanding before they fall behind. And by making data available to parents, they can track their child's progress and participate more fully in their education.

Beyond addressing the needs of individual students, data aids schools in their institutional and administrative functions. School and district leaders rely on data to drive improvement and decision making around curriculum, technology infrastructure, and staffing.

The availability of new types of data also improves researchers' ability to learn about learning. Data from a student's experience in technology-based learning platforms can be precisely tracked, opening the door to more accurately understanding how students move through a curriculum, and at greater scale, than traditional education research is able to achieve.

As data systems become more integrated into the learning and teaching process, we are seeing the impact that they can have on students, teachers, administrators, and policymakers. These systems enable teachers, schools, and districts to make more informed decisions to enhance student learning.

Meanwhile, a growing number of on-line educational services have the ability to enhance learning within the classroom and extend it beyond the school day. Edmodo, which is used by more than 20 million teachers and students world-wide, allows teachers to set up virtual classrooms and then post homework assignments and other content to extend lessons. Khan Academy has more than 5,000 instructional videos and assessments, which allow students of all ages to learn at their own pace in subject areas ranging from pre-algebra to differential equations, from art history to computer science.

With this explosion in on-line resources, there is a large amount of new data being generated by children using these services, which raises valid privacy concerns.

The privacy of student education records is protected under FERPA, the Family Educational Rights and Privacy Act. When those student education records are hosted or analyzed by private companies that are helping districts build data systems to drive improvement, those same FERPA protections still apply.

However, when students use on-line services like Khan Academy—in school or at home—or when teachers use grade and behavior tracking software on their iPads, all of that data are not necessarily covered by FERPA. In those direct interactions between students and software companies, data are being collected to build user profiles, individualize the learning experience, and track progress, but in the cases where FERPA does not apply, it is not always clear what protections exist to guarantee the privacy of those data and ensure companies are not using them to target advertisements at children.

This committee will hear important testimony today about the value that these tailored technological resources provide to students themselves and the importance of ensuring access to data for teachers and researchers seeking to improve education. We'll also hear about the need for consistent privacy policies and current efforts to guarantee the security and privacy of student data.

As we examine the privacy concerns prompted by the rapidly growing education technology sector and the information it collects, it's clear that we must strive to find a balance between privacy and innovation. We must ensure that companies involved in collecting and analyzing student data are not exploiting students' private information for marketing purposes or financial gain. Data are an invaluable tool. Data empowers teachers, guides individualized learning, and informs policy. As we consider where improvements are needed in privacy regulations, we must be sure that we do not compromise the value of student data.

I look forward to hearing from our witnesses.

Thank you very much.

Mr. MEEHAN. Let me thank Ranking Member Loebsack for his opening statement and for his insights. I am also very—oh, let me also remind other Members of the committee that opening statements may be submitted for the record.

[The statements of Ranking Member Thompson, Hon. Jackson Lee, and Hon. Polis follow:]

STATEMENT OF RANKING MEMBER BENNIE G. THOMPSON

JUNE 25, 2014

There is considerable controversy about how we treat the vast amounts of student data created in the education field. Education's large-scale data sets—what scientists refer to as "big data"—are troves of potential knowledge about our students. From education's "big data", teachers can learn instructional methods; textbook writers can adapt their content; and policy makers can make decisions on curriculum guidelines. However, the information technology involved in storing the big data is outpacing the infrastructure and the contractual agreements that school districts currently have in place. Educational data contains sensitive, Personally Identifiable Information about our students. Parents are justifiably concerned about schools' use of their children's student data.

The Family Educational Rights and Privacy Act, or FERPA, was written and has been amended to protect the privacy of student education records. The law applies to all schools that receive funds under an applicable program of the U.S. Department of Education. FERPA gives parents certain rights with respect to access to their children's education records. While the Department of Homeland Security does identify Education as a sub-sector in the National Infrastructure Protection Plan, most of the planning and coordination between the two agencies exists because of physical security and emergency response planning needs in the event of natural or man-made disaster or terroristic events.

What we will hear today is testimony on the implications of the collection, storage, and use of in-depth student data, as managed by local and State school systems, and the Department of Education. The Department of Homeland Security is considered the leader among civilian agencies in developing privacy-protective technologies and policies for handling personal data, and has initiated pilot programs for developing a Federal Department-wide capability to analyze the large sets of data that DHS agencies collect.

As part of this "big data" effort, DHS has brought together stakeholders to find ways to incorporate privacy protections in the management of big data strictly in the dot-gov arena. And DHS has been involved in Federal research efforts as part of the Networking and Information Technology Research and Development program, on data privacy technologies in general, efforts promoted by the White House Office of Science and Technology.

It is possible that the Department's leadership role in the Federal Government's cyber R&D efforts can help provide advanced IT capabilities for the education sector, and other sectors concerned with privacy. There is a huge body of study already underway by academia, educational advocacy, and industry groups to develop and enable a common language for security and privacy policies tailored to students and parents, as well as to organizations and entities that underpin the education environment.

This could potentially help school systems, and parents, that are struggling with contractual or technological or procedural privacy concerns associated with educational "big data". Like with all critical infrastructure networks, we must find a way to work together with schools, nonprofits, and industry to enable parents and educators to make informed decisions and maximize the opportunities that come with rapidly-advancing technology, without comprising our students and learners' privacy and safety.

———

STATEMENT OF HON. SHEILA JACKSON LEE

JUNE 25, 2014

My thanks to Chairman Meehan and Ranking Member Clarke of the Committee on Homeland Security Subcommittee on Cybersecurity, Infrastructure Protection, and Security Technologies as well the Education and the Workforce Committee's Subcommittee on Early Childhood, Elementary, and Secondary Education for holding today's joint hearing "How Data Mining Threatens Student Privacy."

Today's hearing is an opportunity to receive testimony on the issue of student kindergarden through 12th grade data privacy, data mining, confidentiality, and security practices related to cyber-based student and educational IT systems. Members will have the opportunity to hear testimony about how cloud-based databases and other IT technologies, used in K–12 schools are becoming increasingly complex and expansive, prompting an examination of the approaches that protect private student data, who may have access to it, and where and how it is stored.

As the founder member and chair of the Children's Caucus the topic of today's hearing is of great interest to me.

Children often do not enjoy the same rights as adults—they cannot consume alcohol, vote, nor can children enter into contracts.

However, children also have a level of protections in law that are greater than those of adults such as the Children's Online Privacy Protection Act, child labor laws, laws to prevent abuse and neglect and laws regarding education such as the Family and Educational Rights and Privacy Act of 1974 (FERPA).

These laws are is intended to facilitate children having safe and happy childhoods, which means the freedom to make mistakes and learn from those mistakes.

Many children do not grow up the most ideal circumstances and those circumstances should not influence the course of their lives without due cause.

In recent years there have been a number of incidents where the privacy of children has been violated by school districts that are of great concern.

Primary of which is the incident involving the Lower Merion County Pennsylvania School District.

That School District became internationally known when it was disclosed that it deployed spyware to take thousands of images of student while using their school-issued laptops.

Images were taken of students while off school grounds, often went they were at home. Images were captured of not only students, but family members while in intimate settings.

The case was a very emotional and situation for both families and school officials who were unaware of the activities of the technology department that deployed the surveillance system.

Privacy violations of this type have most often occurred in domestic abuse or predator cases. This is the first known case to rise from an incident of a non-judicial decision by a domestic government institution to use this type of surveillance technology in this manner.

Because Federal and State laws had not kept pace with technology there were no laws that address that type of privacy invasion that relied upon still pictures and not full motion video.

Privacy is central to the health and strength of many other rights that we enjoy. Specifically, the First, Fourth, and Fifth Amendments to the Constitution rests on a foundation of privacy protection that allow us to speak as we wish, associate with other and hold our own beliefs free of fear or threats.

Privacy should not nor has it been viewed as a partisan issue.

So the topic of today's hearing is of great concern to me. There cannot be privacy without security, although we can have security without privacy. The digital information age requires that Federal agencies must have cybersecurity for any system that collects, retains, or uses personal information.

Privacy protection and cybersecurity are linked in the work I have done on the topic of privacy. The ability to control who, when, why, and how someone else can gain access to personal information requires security for this reason attention to this issue is central to my strong support for Federal privacy laws.

Although the Homeland Security Committee has no jurisdiction over general education issues there are aspects of today's hearing which do touch upon some our work of the Committee on Homeland such as questions regarding data security.

Each of these children will be part of the workforce which will include the Department of Homeland Security. To the extent data security and privacy is compromised in education settings this may have an impact on the future ability of workers and employers to rely upon Department of Homeland Security programs like e-Verify, TWIC, or air travelers to trust PreCheck programs.

Each of these data collection and use programs requires data non-repudiation.

Data non-repudiation very simply establishes that a person is who they claim to be.

Further, we know from the work of intelligence and National security agencies that adversaries and friends seek as much detailed information on key persons in the Federal Government and influential private-sector business leaders.

Data collection practices regarding student records on children:

- At least 38 States collecting some type of longitudinal student data at the State level, five others are in various stages of development, and the rest are insufficiently transparent to determine.
- At least 32 percent of States collect children's social security numbers.
- At least 22 percent of States record student pregnancies.
- At least 46 percent of States have a mechanism in place to track children's mental health, illnesses, and jail sentences.
- At least, 72 percent of States collect children's family wealth indicators.
- Only 6 States appear to use a third party who restricts the State's access to the student ID numbers, i.e. prevents State access to individual student data.
- Only 18 States have detailed access and use restrictions.
- Only 18 States require database users to enter into confidentiality agreements.
- Only 10 States have data retention policies.
- Forty-nine States make FERPA information accessible on the internet, but for many the information is hard to find, vague, or incomprehensible.

The change in the Family and Educational Rights and Privacy Act of 1974 (FERPA) rule regarding what entities can have access to student records is troubling.

In April 2011, the U.S. Department of Education (ED) issued a notice of proposed rulemaking (NPRM), inviting public comments on its proposed regulations amending the Family and Educational Rights and Privacy Act of 1974 (FERPA).

The final rule removed limitations prohibiting educational institutions and agencies from disclosing student Personally Identifiable Information, without first obtaining student or parental consent.

The change in FERPA regulations redefined FERPA definitions regarding "authorized representative," "education program," and "directory information." The new definition gave non-governmental actors increased access to student personal data.

I am not opposed to the collection data on students regarding their lives, education or well-being for education purposes.

I am however, strong object to use of student record information outside of the purpose of the collection and the lack of control over those records that parents may have in limiting access and use for non-official purposes.

Student record data should be limited to education purposes with the exception of uses related to the protection of the well-being of the child and their family.

Data brokers a new business model that buys and sells a wide range of personal information would find great value in have unlimited control and use of personal identifiable information—the more sensitive that information—the more value that information.

Too often the opportunity to limit additional uses of personal information on students requires a parent or guardian to act, when allowed to control the use of their child's education records.

This will mean that students whose families are not as equipped or knowledgeable of the data collection, use, and retention polices regarding student records will likely have their information retained and used, which can have serious consequences for the opportunities they may have in the future.

Personal Identifiable Information should be protected by fair information practices no matter the age of the person whose information is collected.

I strongly believe that our children are our Nation's most precious resource and their futures should not be limited or influenced by a permanent government record that contains unprotected information from their earliest years throughout their work like.

I yield back.

Thank you.

STATEMENT OF HON. JARED POLIS

JUNE 25, 2014

Recently, concerns about the increasing collection and use of student data in schools have come to the forefront in local education debates. The fall of the non-profit education database, inBloom, as well as the hearing today titled, "How Data Mining Threatens Our Children" are evidence of widespread consternation from the left and the right.

I believe that security and privacy are critical, yet manageable concerns. We should not dismiss the power of using data to improve classroom instruction; simply develop best practices to ensure that data is used responsibly. Data can be a powerful tool to provide parents with meaningful information about their child's progress, connect students and families with personalized learning opportunities, and create high-quality materials and tools that can bring our education system into the 21st Century.

InBloom's demise raised important concerns about the appropriate privacy and security precautions necessary to protect beneficial student data in an increasingly technological school environment. That's why I am urging industry, parents, and teachers to come together to address these concerns with a set of expectations and commitments on how to best protect and secure our children's data, while enjoying the benefits of more personalized learning.

When I am back home in Colorado, I hear from parents who are rightly concerned about data security, but optimistic about improving their children's educational opportunities. They worry about where their student data is stored, whether it is secure, and who it is shared with. They worry about a pervasive "permanent record." They worry that advertising companies may inappropriately target their children and somehow profit on their decisions in what should be a safe and secure school environment. At the same time, they want for their children to succeed in an increasingly connected digital world. They want to know how their children are developing, and what they can do to help. And they want to be able to make informed choices about the best schooling options for their children.

Parents want what is best for their children, and deserve transparency about what is happening in their schools. Unfortunately, the intersection of the Family Educational Rights and Privacy Act (FERPA), Children's Online Privacy and Protection Act (COPPA), a growing number of State laws, district policies, vendor contracts, and privacy policies make it very difficult for them to have confidence that their children's data is being used solely to advance their education. Lately, these concerns have moved from hesitation to outright opposition to the collection and use of student data.

While opposition is mounting for valid reasons, we must recognize the promise of digital learning and the opportunities that collecting, analyzing, and utilizing student data, appropriately, presents to personalized education. I have experienced the power of digital learning as the former chair of the State board of education in Colorado, and know that timely, relevant, and private information about student performance can be an important tool to ensure that our education system is able to identify student's strengths and challenges and intervene appropriately.

I am concerned that a purely political reaction to legitimate privacy concerns threatens to derail the potential of digital learning and years of progress in personalizing education. Federal legislation is an option, but may not be able to provide a nuanced solution in such a complex and emerging field.

That's why I, along with Representative Luke Messer are calling on industry leaders, parents, and teachers to come together around a set of effective and appropriate expectations and commitments on data privacy in schools. These standards should be rigorous, but adaptable; comprehensive, yet easily comprehensible for parents to understand what is occurring in their schools. That is why a few weeks ago, we were honored to convene a group of industry and educational leaders to discuss the topic, and are pleased with the group's progress during the first meeting. We are calling on these groups to develop a transparent set of expectations and commitments in time for back-to-school.

Ensuring the right balance between privacy and innovation in education is a critical, bipartisan issue that will pave the way for the next generation of students to thrive. I am looking forward to working with industry, parents, and teachers to achieve this balance, and make a promise of which we can all be proud.

Mr. MEEHAN. I am also very grateful for what is a very distinguished panel of some real experts who understand and have spent a great deal of time looking at this issue from multiple factors. So what we really hope we are able to do is encourage the kind of insight and give and take to help us best understand how we might both understand the challenges in this issue and act accordingly to protect appropriately the privacy of our students.

Ms. CLARKE. Mr. Chairman.

Mr. MEEHAN. Yes.

Ms. CLARKE. Before you proceed, I would like to request unanimous consent for Ms. Bonamici of the Education and the Workforce Committee to join us in the hearing today.

Mr. MEEHAN. Without objection, so ordered.

Ms. CLARKE. Thank you.

Mr. MEEHAN. Thank you for being here, Ms. Bonamici.

I will briefly introduce each of the distinguished panel members today. First, to my left, is Mr. Joel Reidenberg. He is the Stanley D. and Nikki Waxberg chair, and professor of law and founding academic director at the Center on Law and Information Policy at Fordham University School of Law. Mr. Reidenberg is an expert on information technology law and policy, and his current research examines privacy in public information surveillance, privacy in cloud computing in purchase schools, and the impact of patents on the smartphone industry.

Next to Mr. Reidenberg is Mr. Mark MacCarthy. Mr. MacCarthy is a vice president of public policy for the Software and Information Industry Association. Mr. MacCarthy directs SIIA's public privacy initiatives in the areas of intellectual property enforcement, information privacy, cybersecurity, cloud computing, and the promotion of education technology. The Software and Information Industry Association is the principle trade association for the software and digital content industry, providing global services in Government relations, business development, corporate education, and intellectual property protection.

Next is Ms. Joyce Popp. Ms. Popp is the chief investment officer for the Idaho Department of Education. One of her key focuses since joining the State department of education in July 2009 has been the design management and security of the data collection process and the use of data. Prior to joining the State department of education, Ms. Joyce had over 30 years experience in management within the high-tech industry, leading large teams in the creation, design, and support of data systems and information exchange.

Last is Mr. Thomas Murray. Mr. Murray is the State and district digital learning policy advocacy director for the Alliance for Excellent Education. The Alliance for Excellent Education is a D.C.-based National policy and advocacy organization dedicated to en-

16

suring that all students graduate from high school. Mr. Murray works alongside State education departments, corporations, and school districts around the country to implement digital learning. As a former school principal, Mr. Murray has been invested regarding proper technology in fusion and personalized professional learning. He is the founder of #Edchat, a weekly educational technology twitter-forum, and has a weekly radio show on the BAM Radio Network.

I want to let each of the witnesses know that your full written statements will appear in the record. We are limited, or try to stay as closely as we can, to 5 minutes to testify. You are dealing with a weighty, a meaty, and important subject, so I will ask. You all have impressive backgrounds and resumes, and I will take official notice of your impressive qualifications. So with the time that you have, if you can, I would like to ask if you would dig right into the substance of your observations on this issue because you have a great deal to share with us in time that we make available to you.

So at this point in time, the Chairman recognizes Mr. Reidenberg for your comments.

STATEMENT OF JOEL R. REIDENBERG, STANLEY D. AND NIKKI WAXBERG CHAIR AND PROFESSOR OF LAW, FOUNDING ACADEMIC DIRECTOR, CENTER OF LAW AND INFORMATION POLICY, FORDHAM UNIVERSITY SCHOOL OF LAW

Mr. REIDENBERG. Good morning, Mr. Chairman, Ranking Members and distinguished Members of the subcommittees. Thank you very much for inviting me to testify this morning. It is truly an honor and a privilege to be able to address these issues. My testimony is going to draw on the Fordham study, that the Chairman mentioned, that I directed addressing privacy in cloud computing in public schools. I hope that this study might be included with the record of the committee hearing today.

I am joined today by two of my co-authors from the study, Cameron Russell and Tom Norton. But I am giving my own views as an academic expert and I am not representing those of any organization. I am gonna spend my time summarizing four of the key points from the written statement. The first is that schools—essentially, every school district in the United States is outsourcing student information. Our study found there were—95 percent of the school districts did this.

Schools are sending data to third parties for a whole series of very positive reasons: Data-driven educational goals; reporting obligations; cost savings; instructional opportunities. We found in our study that there was a tremendous diversity in type of services and the service providers themselves. The services ranged from classroom instructional functions, reporting functions, data mining, guidance for college and career counseling, IT hosting, special services like transportation and cafeteria management. The number of vendors are staggering.

It is a very wide range from large companies to small companies. There is an enough quantity of information that is being transferred by school districts. It is not simply the traditional school record, the grades or the transcripts. It includes things like homework assignments, essays, fitness profiles, family financial records and financial status, lunchroom purchases, whether a child blinks while he is reading. All of these sorts of things are being transferred as children use on-line services in schools and as schools rely on third parties to perform some of their functions.

The second point is that Federal educational privacy law fails to protect the student information. There are essentially three statutes that I believe are relevant in this context. FERPA is one, a 40-year-old statute; the Children's Online Privacy Protection Act that requires parental consent when data is gathered directly from children on-line under the age of 13; and the Pupil Privacy Protection Amendment that addresses taking surveys of children in schools. FERPA is essentially the baseline that everyone speaks of. But FERPA only applies to educational institutions. It is a funding statute.

It does not apply to the vendors. It only applies narrowly to what are defined as educational records. The Supreme Court, in its one decision interpreting that provision of FERPA, seems to think an educational record is only the type of data that would have been held in a principal's file cabinet. So when you look at the statute itself from 1974, it is a pre-computer era statute. COPPA has some application if children are on-line in schools. The school districts can, in certain instances, consent as though they were parents. But then what happens when the child moves from school to home and works on the same application? It has been an instructional tool.

States are beginning, across the country, to look to fill some of these gaps. But contracts would be the only source of true protection. What our study shows is that schools essentially routinely relinquish their students' privacy when they contract with outside vendors, and parents are kept in the dark. We heard from the Chairman's opening statement, 20 percent of the schools have no policies on adopting technologies. Seventy-five percent of the districts failed to inform parents that they are outsourcing their children's data.

The contract practices, on the whole, are terrible. Many of the contracts allow vendors to unilaterally change the terms. They don't block the sale or marketing of data. Forty percent of the hosting agreements fail to require any data security. Twenty-five percent of the classroom programs are free programs; they don't charge school districts money. Instead, the school districts essentially pay with the student's privacy. The data is being monetized.

My fourth point is that strong and effective privacy protections are essential. Because without them, if we persist with the status quo, all of the educational policies that we want to achieve based on data-driven decision-making, they will fail. Parents will object to the use of these technologies. There will be scandals, there will be problems that will shut down rather than carefully nuance how to treat the data privacy issues. We have seen this in New York State, for example, with the inBloom project. InBloom is a $100 million project, it is a platform that would enable data sharing between schools and vendors. It shut down over the privacy concerns.

In my prepared statement, I make four recommendations for Congress to consider. I see my time has expired so I will perhaps leave those recommendations for you to see in a written statement, and we can answer—I will answer any questions on them during the following period.

Thank you.

[The prepared statement of Mr. Reidenberg follows:]

PREPARED STATEMENT OF JOEL R. REIDENBERG

JUNE 25, 2014

Good morning Chairman Meehan, Representative Clarke, Chairman Rokita, Representative Loebsach, and distinguished Members of the subcommittees. I would like to thank you for the invitation to testify today on this critical privacy issue for our Nation's school children.

My name is Joel Reidenberg. I am here today as an academic expert on student information and privacy. I hold the Stanley D. and Nikki Waxberg chair at Fordham University where I am a professor of law and the academic director of the Center on Law and Information Policy ("Fordham CLIP"). I am also just finishing my term as the inaugural Microsoft Visiting Professor of Information Technology Policy at Princeton University.

As a law scholar, I have written and lectured extensively on data privacy law and policy. I am a member of the American Law Institute where I serve as an adviser to the *Restatement of the Law Third on Information Privacy Principles.* I am a former chair of the Association of American Law School's Section on Defamation and Privacy and have served as an expert adviser on data privacy issues for the Federal Trade Commission, the European Commission, and during the 103rd and 104th Congresses for the Office of Technology Assessment. I have also served as a special assistant attorney general for the State of Washington in connection with privacy litigation.

Of relevance to today's hearing, I directed the research study "Privacy and Cloud Computing in Public Schools" (Dec. 2013) ["Fordham CLIP Study"] that provides a benchmark analysis of the processing of student information by on-line vendors and that also documents the current legal risks surrounding student privacy.[1] Two members of the Fordham CLIP research team, N. Cameron Russell, Fordham CLIP's executive director, and Thomas B. Norton, Fordham CLIP's privacy fellow, accompany me here today.

In appearing today, I am testifying as an academic expert and my views should not be attributed to any organization with which I am or have been affiliated.

My testimony today draws specifically from the Fordham CLIP Study. I will address a number of our key findings.

1. Schools are uniformly transferring vast amounts of student information to on-line third parties for many varied purposes.

School districts across the country are rapidly embracing evolving on-line technologies to meet data-driven educational goals, satisfy reporting obligations, realize information technology cost savings, and take advantage of new instructional opportunities.

The Fordham CLIP Study found that 95% of public schools in the United States use on-line services that involve the transfer of student information to third parties. Schools use these services for a myriad of purposes that the Fordham CLIP Study categorized as follows:
- Data analytics functions
- Student reporting functions
- Classroom functions
- Guidance functions
- Special school functions (e.g., transportation services)
- Hosting, maintenance, and back-up functions.[2]

These on-line services involve the collection and transfer of enormous quantities of student information to third-party commercial organizations including school records, homework essays, fitness profiles, and even lunchroom purchases.

---

[1] Joel R. Reidenberg, N. Cameron Russell, Jordan Kovnot, Thomas B. Norton, Ryan Cloutier, Daniela Alvarado, *Privacy and Cloud Computing in Public Schools* (Dec. 2013) available at *http://law.fordham.edu/k12cloudprivacy* [hereinafter "Fordham CLIP Study"]. I also directed an earlier study, *Children's Educational Records and Privacy: A Study of Elementary and Secondary School State Reporting Systems* (Fordham CLIP: Oct. 28, 2009) *http://law.fordham.edu/childrensprivacy* and testified on that work in a hearing before the House Committee on Education and Labor during the 111th Congress.

[2] Fordham CLIP Study, at pp. 17–18.

2. Federal education privacy law fails to protect student information in a vast range of commercial computing services used by schools.

Three Federal privacy statutes address student information that may be collected by and from schools: The Family Educational Rights and Privacy Act of 1974 [3] ("FERPA"), the Children's Online Privacy Protection Act [4] ("COPPA"), and the Protection of Pupil Rights Amendment [5] ("PPRA").

FERPA is the oldest and best-known educational privacy statute. The statute seeks to provide confidentiality to student data, but only covers "educational records" in a very narrow sense (e.g., transcripts).[6] The statute also specifically exempts "directory information," including a student's name, address, date of birth, telephone number, age, sex, and weight from confidentiality obligations.[7] Most significantly, FERPA was written 40 years ago before public schools had computers, let alone internet access. As acknowledged by the Department of Education, the applicability of FERPA to typical on-line school services is questionable at best.[8]

The other statutes, COPPA (addressing parental consent for on-line collection of data directly from children younger than 13) and PPRA (primarily addressing the use of data collected from in-school surveys and some marketing activities), similarly suffer from significant protection gaps in the context of cloud computing, that the Fordham CLIP Study explains.

Many cloud services used by schools are, thus, completely outside the protections of these statutes. For example, when a middle school uses a cloud service provider to offer young teens self-assessment tests that give scores to their language or math levels, those scores will not likely be protected by the Federal statutes: They are not FERPA "educational records" because they are not used for the middle schooler's transcript grade, they do not require COPPA parental consent, and they fall outside the PPRA categories of protection. Thus, there is no statutory obligation of confidentiality.

Another example comes from special school functions: Schools are now using third-party on-line service providers to manage payments for the school cafeteria. When a child buys a meal in the school cafeteria, the information about the child's eating habits will not have privacy protection.

Another important point to note is that FERPA does not apply to vendors. By its terms, FERPA only applies to educational agencies and institutions that are recipients of Federal funds.[9] FERPA does not provide a private right of action,[10] and the only sanction available under FERPA is the denial of Federal educational funds by the Department of Education. The Department has never issued such an order. Thus, under Federal law, legal protection for student privacy will only come from the contractual terms in agreements between schools and vendors.

States, however, are increasingly concerned about the commercial sale of student information. According to recent reports, over 30 States across the country have bills at various stages of enactment to address student privacy on-line. These bills do not generally address the full range of issues and would establish different protections for students in different States.

3. The Fordham CLIP study documents that schools routinely relinquish student privacy when they contract for on-line services and parents are kept in the dark.

In the absence of statutory rights, schools can protect student privacy through their contracts with on-line service providers. The Fordham CLIP Study, however, demonstrates that contracts between schools and vendors often fail to establish legal rights that protect student information. Schools essentially relinquish their students' privacy in the cloud. And, at the same time, schools routinely fail to inform parents that their children's data is sent to third parties.

Among the findings, the Fordham CLIP Study reported that:
- *Technology governance controls are absent.*—20% of school districts have no policies on the vetting and adoption of information technology services by teachers and staff.

---

[3] 20 U.S.C. § 1232g.
[4] 15 U.S.C. §§ 6501–6506.
[5] 20 U.S.C. § 1232h.
[6] See *Owasso Independent School District* v. *Falvo,* 534 U.S. 426 (2002).
[7] 20 U.S.C. § 1232g(a)(5)(A).
[8] Dept. of Educ., Protecting Student Privacy While Using Online Educational Services: Requirements and Best Practices, PTAC FAQ3 (Feb. 2014) *http://ptac.ed.gov/document/protecting-student-privacy-while-using-online-educational-services* (the Department wrote: "Is student information used in online educational services protected by FERPA? It depends.").
[9] 20 U.S.C. § 1232g(a).
[10] *Gonzaga Univ.* v. *Doe,* 536 U.S. 273 (2002).

- *Transparency is missing.*—75% of districts did not inform parents that their children's data was being released to on-line service providers, and districts do not readily make their agreements publicly accessible.
- *Legal compliance is not working.*—COPPA is frequently ignored; FERPA notices are rare.
- *Contract practices are disturbing.*—Over 75% of the agreements fail to specify a legitimate purpose for processing student data, vendors are routinely able to modify the privacy terms on a unilateral basis, and schools fail to keep adequate documentation of their contracts.
- *Student data may be sold for advertising and marketing.*—Fewer than 7% of agreements explicitly prohibit the sale or marketing of student information, though higher percentages of agreements have general restrictions on re-disclosure. Without a contractual prohibition, vendors are free to sell the student information.
- *Data security protections are poor.*—40% of hosting agreements, like many other categories, fail to require any data security and, depending on the type of service, 33% or more of the agreements fail to require the deletion of student information at contract termination.[11]

These findings present a very disturbing set of risks to the privacy of our Nation's student information. A permanent record may now indeed follow a child from elementary school through adulthood. For example, the company ConnectEdu held data on over 20 million students and offered a product called K12 Early Warning Indicator.[12] The product sought to label students with the goal of identifying and helping at-risk students. But, the lack of privacy protection means that the label may now follow the child indefinitely. Worse still, the company is now in bankruptcy and the Federal Trade Commission had to make a special filing in the hope that it could persuade the bankruptcy judge not to sell off to the highest bidder all the student data held by the bankrupt company.[13]

Similarly, student data becomes fuel for commercial uses. In some contexts, such as those involving classroom functions, 25% of the school contracts involved no financial payments. This likely means that these vendors are monetizing the student information to fund the services they provide. In other words, school districts are paying for services with their students' privacy rather than cash. This was dramatically illustrated by disclosures in the law suit against Google for its scanning of student email. Originally, Google represented to educational institutions that it did not scan student email for commercial advertising.[14] As it turned out, Google was profiling students based on their email.[15] In a policy change announced on April 30, 2014, Google said that it would no longer "collect or use student data in Apps for Education services for advertising purposes."[16] Google remains silent, however, on scanning email and profiling student users for other commercial purposes and partnerships with education technology companies. Google is not alone. The other companies that offer education technology products without fees are or will be trading on student privacy.

4. Without strong and effective privacy protections for student information, data-driven educational policies will fail and parents will oppose new instructional methods.

The responsibility for placing student privacy at risk through these observed practices is complex. Federal laws such as the No Child Left Behind Act and the American Recovery and Reinvestment Act of 2009 required schools to create and report detailed student information. Innovations in technology and incentives for data mining create new demands for student information. Yet, at the same time, education

---

[11] See Fordham CLIP Study, Executive Summary, pp. 1–2.

[12] See ConnectEdu, About Us *http://connectedu.com/about-us* (stating the company had data on 20 million "registered learners"); ConnectEdu, What does K12 Early Warning do for you, *http://207.127.11.51/products-k12earlywarning-features.html* ("locate students at risk").

[13] See Federal Trade Commission Letter From Jessica L. Rich, Director of the Bureau of Consumer Protection, Filed With the Bankruptcy Court for the Southern District of New York—in In re ConnectEDU, Inc., No. 14–11238 (Bankr. S.D.N.Y.) (May 22, 2014) *http://www.ftc.gov/system/files/documents/public_statements/311501/140523connecteducommltr.pdf.*

[14] See Jeff Gould, Google admits data mining student emails in its free education apps, SafeGov.Org (Jan. 31., 2014) *http://safegov.org/2014/1/31/google-admits-data-mining-student-emails-in-its-free-education-apps* (quoting a pre-2013 Google FAQ saying "note that there is no ad-related scanning or processing in Google Apps for Education").

[15] See Michele Molnar, Google Abandons Scanning of Student Email, Education Week, Apr. 20, 2014, *http://blogs.edweek.org/edweek/marketplacek12/2014/04/google_abandons_scanning_of_student_email_accounts.html.*

[16] Protecting students with Google Apps for Education, Apr. 30, 2014 *http://googleenterprise.blogspot.com/2014/04/protecting-students-with-google-apps.html.*

privacy laws have not been modernized to keep up, and our research revealed that schools were not equipped to address these issues effectively.

Data collection and use to inform and improve student learning is critical to making education successful in the United States. But so is the long-term health of our children's privacy. More often than not, school districts poorly understood the data transfers and privacy implications of the on-line services they use.[17] Other than the largest districts with legal offices, few had either the expertise or the ability to negotiate contract terms that were drafted by vendors.

As a result, today's status quo is an unstable and contentious environment for education technology. The recent failure of inBloom, a $100 million venture to develop a platform for education data, demonstrates that privacy risks will shut down programs when public concerns are not addressed effectively.[18] If privacy is not adequately and transparently addressed, parents will oppose the use of education technologies for fear of their children's safety.

Strong and effective privacy protections for student information are essential for data-driven educational policies to succeed.

RECOMMENDATIONS

There are a number of steps Congress can take to restore and assure the privacy of student information:

(1) Modernize FERPA to protect and limit the use of all student information whether held by schools or vendors—including a prohibition on non-educational uses of student information and graduated enforcement remedies such as private rights of action.

(2) Require that the processing of student data under any Federally-financed educational program be prohibited unless there is a written agreement spelling out the purposes for the processing, restricting the processing to the minimum amount of data necessary for those purposes, restricting the processing to permissible educational uses, mandating data security, requiring data deletion at the end of the contract, and providing for schools' audit and inspection rights with respect to vendors.

(3) Require that States adopt an oversight mechanism for the collection and use of student data by local and State educational agencies. A Chief Privacy Officer in State departments of education is essential to provide transparency to the public, assistance for local school districts to meet their privacy responsibilities, and oversight for compliance with privacy requirements.

(4) Provide support to the Department of Education and to the research community to address privacy in the context of rapidly-evolving educational technologies, including support for a clearing center to assist schools and vendors find appropriate best practices for their needs.

Thank you again for the opportunity to participate in this hearing and for your consideration of my testimony.

Mr. MEEHAN. Yes, you will have an opportunity to elaborate, I think, on some of those in response to the questions, or to open the door to some of those in responses to any questions you may have.

The Chairman now recognizes Mr. MacCarthy.

Mr. MacCarthy, I am gonna ask that you push your button so that we can pick up your voice.

Mr. MACCARTHY. Now do you have it?

Mr. MEEHAN. I have it.

---

[17] See Fordham CLIP Study, p. 15 (describing districts' lack of knowledge of their own agreements); Stephanie Simon, Data mining your children, Politico, May 15, 2014 *http://www.politico.com/story/2014/05/data-mining-your-children-106676.html* ("school administrators . . . don't know which digital tools individual teachers are using in the classroom.").

[18] See Benjamin Herold, inBloom to shut down amid growing privacy concerns, Education Week, Apr. 21, 2014 *http://blogs.edweek.org/edweek/DigitalEducation/2014/04/inbloom_to_shut_down_amid_growing_data_privacy_concerns.html*.

STATEMENT OF MARK MAC CARTHY, VICE PRESIDENT, PUBLIC POLICY, SOFTWARE AND INFORMATION INDUSTRY ASSOCIATION

Mr. MACCARTHY. Excellent. Thank you. My name is Mark MacCarthy and I am with Software and Information Industry Association. On behalf of SIIA and our member companies—many of whom are involved in providing educational services to schools—I want to thank you for having me here to testify on this important topic. I want to thank you for your thoughtful opening statements on this topic.

Mr. Chairman, Ranking Members, the effective use of educational technology and student information is essential for improving student learning, for empowering parents and, ultimately, for ensuring the competitiveness of the United States in a global environment. Let me take a few minutes to explain some of the uses of technology and student information, and how it is transforming American education.

They are enabling multiple approaches to learning to address each individual student's individual learning style, their abilities, their pace, their interests. Data-powered course-ware helps teachers deliver customized lessons to each individual student. Predictive analytics are allowing students and teachers to identify students at risk of failing in a particular course or even of dropping out of school entirely. Data-driven technology is empowering parents, allowing them to access information about their children's educational progress and communicating more effectively and actively with their teachers.

Cloud computing is enhancing school capacity by providing more data access, enhanced data management, powerful analytics, and improved security. The scale of cloud computing enables greater expertise and more investment in information security. The list goes on but, in sum, educational technology is allowing schools to identify students at risk, to personalize learning, to improve communication with parents, to modify their operations better and more efficiently, and to inform their decision making.

Now, of course, we recognize that there are important questions being asked about data privacy. I would like to address three essential ways in which student data is being protected. First is Federal law. Federal law establishes a strong framework that restricts the use of student information to educational purposes. FERPA requires that identifiable information shared with service providers without parental consent or without student consent, must be used solely for institutional services and functions that would otherwise be performed by school officials. It must be used only for educational purposes.

Now, FERPA covers educational records. But educators and service providers treat all identifiable student information with the same high level of privacy protection. While FERPA is 40 years old, its regulations have been updated for the digital age, including student privacy guidance for on-line services released just this year. The Children's Online Privacy Protection Act offers further protections for children under the age of 13.

The bottom line is that if an outside party wants to use student information for non-educational purposes, it is required by law to get the consent of the parent or the student to do so.

So that is the first level of protection, Federal law. The second level is contracts. Student data is also protected by contract. Service providers are bound by the contracts they enter into with schools. Here, frankly, we owe Professor Reidenberg a debt of gratitude, both the industry and the educators, for drawing attention to the limitations on those contracts and the need to work together to improve them.

The third level of protection is the efforts by SIIA and other stakeholders to enhance student data protection. Service providers are continuously reviewing and improving data policies, procedures, and technologies, and are guided, in part, by SIIA's recently-released best practices. The Consortium for School Networking, representing school technology officers, has released a tool kit for protecting student privacy. We appreciate the recent leadership from Representatives Polis and Messer in assembling stakeholders to engage in collective efforts to improve student privacy.

While it makes sense for public policies to be reviewed, we do not think that new Federal student privacy legislation is necessary at this time. The current legal framework and industry practices maintain local decision-making and adequately protect student privacy. New legislation creates substantial risks of harm to the innovative use of information that is essential for improving education for all students, and ensuring that U.S. economic strength in an increasingly global competitive environment is maintained.

I would be happy to answer any questions you might have.

[The prepared statement of Mr. MacCarthy follows:]

PREPARED STATEMENT OF MARK MACCARTHY

JUNE 25, 2014

On behalf of the Software & Information Industry Association (SIIA) and our member high-tech companies, thank you for inviting me to testify today. I am Mark MacCarthy, SIIA's vice president of public policy. SIIA commends Chairman Meehan and Rokita, Ranking Members Clarke and Loebsack and your respective committees for holding this hearing to examine student privacy in the digital age.

SIIA is the principal trade association for the software and digital content industry. Many of SIIA's 800 member high-tech companies partner with schools and universities across the country to develop and deliver learning software applications, digital content, web services and related technologies and services that meet teaching, learning, and enterprise management needs. All SIIA members depend on the Nation's schools for a skilled, high-tech workforce.

Modern information technologies play an increasingly essential role in our education system. SIIA agrees that the effective use of student information to improve learning is concomitant with the obligation to safeguard student data privacy and security. This will require a continued and enhanced trust framework between the triad of stakeholders—parents and schools; schools and service providers; and service providers and parents.

My testimony today will address three questions:
• What are some of the ways students, teachers, and schools use technology and leverage data to improve education?
• What are the current policies and evolving practices protecting student privacy and data security?
• Is there a need for new Federal student privacy legislation?

I. USE OF TECHNOLOGY AND STUDENT INFORMATION IN SCHOOLS

As we move from an industrial-age era model to a customized education model, technology is increasingly mission-critical to making certain all students receive a world-class education, and our Nation competes in the global economy. International assessment results and high-tech job openings demonstrate the challenge of ensuring students are college- and career-ready, including with the STEM (science, technology, engineering, and math) and other 21st Century skills needed to succeed in this knowledge-based economy.

From adaptive learning software to class scheduling applications to on-line learning, technologies are enhancing student access and opportunity and enabling administrative operations. Many of these technologies are based on the effective use of student information for educational purposes. As such, technology and data systems are increasingly essential to supporting students, families, and educators—providing operational efficiencies, informing practice, and personalizing student learning.

Some of the ways the use of educational technology and student information can enable school operations and improve student learning include:

1. *Help Meet the Needs of All Students.*—Technology enables multiple approaches to learning to effectively address each student's individual learning style, abilities, pace, and interests. Through embedded assessment and adaptive content, today's data-powered courseware helps teachers deliver lessons and content in the modality, complexity, and representation to meet every student's unique needs, rather than teaching to the mean. Predictive analytics can also identify students at risk of dropping out of school. Timely identification enables schools to intervene early in the process.

2. *Facilitate Communication and Collaboration.*—Participation in a variety of controlled virtual and learning communities with peers and experts inspires students and teachers to discover, explore, guide, and collaborate. Parents can access information and curriculum, and communicate with teachers in more convenient and powerful ways to support their children's learning.

3. *Manage the Education Enterprise.*—Like businesses, schools are harnessing technology to manage core organizational tasks from accounting to human resources to scheduling. Through data management and analysis tools, administrators can identify performance gaps and effective practices, thus enabling more informed decisions to operate the school more efficiently and effectively.

The recent Obama White House report on data and privacy highlights two complementary main benefits of data in education: Personalized learning and research to enhance understanding about learning. It reads, in part: "Data from a student's experience . . . can be precisely tracked, opening the door to understanding how students move through a learning trajectory with greater fidelity, and at greater scale . . . ". The opportunity is to use this data-driven understanding to customize student instruction and curriculum based on each student's unique needs.

As outlined above, an essential part of the technology-enabled changes to practices in our schools is the collection, use, and sharing of student information for educational purposes. Our educational system has long collected and used student data to operate and inform educational practices, and has routinely done so by using third-party service providers.

Today, new technologies like cloud computing are enhancing school capacity in ways not otherwise possible by providing anytime/anywhere data access, enhanced data management functionality, powerful data analytics, and improved security. The scale of cloud computing enables great expertise and investments in security, which includes predicting and identifying against external threats such as hackers or malware and putting in place the most sophisticated data security technologies. In addition, cloud security guards against more traditional threats such as fire or unlocked file cabinets whereby the technology provides a protection not possible through traditional methods. These tools and techniques allow educators to manage more data in more cost-effective, secure, and sophisticated ways to inform instruction and enhance school productivity.

We can think of these cloud data systems like a safety deposit box—your valuables are in a bank, but only you have the key and decide who gets access. For many data systems, the provider houses the data and provides data tools, but access is controlled by education administrators with the digital key.

The result of advanced data management and analysis tools is the ability for school systems to better identify students at risk of failure, identify the lessons that best meet each and every student's unique needs, inform decision making, and enhance operations. The goal is to translate data into actionable information so we can be smarter as an educational system about how to meet the needs of each student based on understanding of what is most effective with students like me. We should want our students, families, and educators to have all the relevant information, while making sure it is used appropriately for educational purposes and that student data privacy is protected.

II. CURRENT FRAMEWORK OF STUDENT PRIVACY PRACTICES AND PROTECTIONS

Schools and service providers have a shared responsibility to safeguard the privacy and security of student information. One way they do this is by limiting the collection and uses of student personal information to legitimate educational purposes. They have policies and procedures in place to prevent unauthorized use.

Federal law establishes a framework that restricts the collection and use of student information to what is necessary to accomplish legitimate educational purposes.

The Family Educational Rights and Privacy Act (FERPA) requires that:
• personally identifiable information shared with service providers be limited to uses otherwise performed by the school's own employees,
• the provider be under direct control of the school, and
• the information can only be used for educational purposes.

In addition, the Children's Online Privacy Protection Act (COPPA) requires consent for child-directed on-line and mobile collectors of personal information from children under the age of 13, both inside and outside of schools, and prohibits the use of information for behavioral advertising. COPPA requires the operator to provide the school with full notice of its collection, use, and disclosure practices.

FERPA and COPPA require parental consent if the school shares personal student information with third parties for non-educational purposes. These laws also require parental consent if the operator wants to use or disclose the information for its own commercial purposes beyond those related to the provision of services to the school.

In addition, the Protection of Pupil Rights Amendment (PPRA) requires parental notice and opportunity to opt out of activities involving the use of personal information collected from students for marketing and advertising purposes unrelated to the educational purpose for which it was collected.

The U.S. Department of Education has provided some examples of how these rules work in practice to protect student privacy. In its recently-released guidance on protecting student privacy while using on-line educational services, the Department of Education advised that a service provider such as a provider of email service or cafeteria service is not permitted to use student information to target ads to students because this use does not "constitute a legitimate educational interest."

Service providers are also bound by contract and are subject to significant penalties for unauthorized disclosure of personal student information, including a ban on providing services for up to 5 years. And there's a market incentive: If service providers do not live up to their responsibilities, they will lose the confidence of their customers.

In short, school service providers do not have an independent role in the school system. They cannot just use personal student information as they see fit. School service providers collect personal student information only with the explicit approval of the schools and agencies that they work for. They use this information only for the purpose authorized by those educational institutions.

SIIA recognizes questions and concerns raised by some parents, educators, and policy makers. SIIA agrees that the obligation to safeguard student data privacy and security means that continued review and enhancements are needed in the framework of our policies, practices, and technologies.

Stakeholders are responding to recent questions and concerns:
• Service providers continuously review and improve data policies, procedures, and technologies.
• SIIA has released industry "Best Practices for the Safeguarding of Student Information Privacy and Security for Providers of School Services" that address educational purpose, transparency, school authorization, data security, and data breach notification *(http://bit.ly/SIIAstudentPrivacyBP)*.
• The Federal Government recently updated regulations and guidance for FERPA and COPPA specific to on-line educational services.
• The Consortium for School Networking (CoSN), representing school CTOs, recently released a toolkit for protecting privacy, "Considerations When Choosing an Online Service Provider for your School System."
• School districts are instituting supplemental agreements with their vendors that further specify restrictive data use, security, and confidentiality terms.
• School districts and non-profits are developing criteria for the review of apps, websites, and cloud-based software, and sharing the criteria and review results.

These policies and agreements enhance a framework of laws and practices that has been highly effective through the years in safeguarding student privacy and data security.

III. THE NEED FOR FEDERAL STUDENT PRIVACY LEGISLATION

SIIA and our member companies agree with the need to review and improve public policies as needed. However, we do not think that new Federal legislation is needed at this time. The current legal framework and industry practices adequately protect student privacy. Moreover, new legislation creates substantial risks of harm to the innovative use of information that is essential to improving education for all students and ensuring U.S. economic strength in an increasingly competitive global environment. These risks include:

- New legislative requirements would not provide local communities and school officials with sufficient flexibility, and Government actions intended to create a privacy and security floor would instead unintentionally create a digital learning ceiling.
- Policies that are overly restrictive or make impractical requirements would have a chilling effect on schools and service providers that would stifle the emergence of personalized learning environments and the effective use of predictive analytics to improve student learning.

SIIA agrees with the Obama administration's May 2014 report on data and privacy, which called for "Responsible Educational Innovation in the Digital Age," including that "Students and their families need robust protection against current and emerging harms, but they also deserve access to the learning advancements enabled by technology that promise to empower all students to reach their full potential."

Similarly, the Aspen Institute Task Force on Learning and the internet's recent report, "Learner at the Center of a Networked World," cautions that "Approaches to providing safety online that are defensive and fear-based are often ineffective and can have the unintended consequence of significantly restricting learning opportunities for young people." SIIA agrees with the Aspen Institute that technology "can be part of the solution by helping create trusted environments."

SIIA recently issued "Policy Guidelines for Building a Student Privacy Trust Framework" (*http://bit.ly/SIIAStudentPrivacyPolicyGuidelines*) that I ask be included in the record of the hearing.

Finally, while this hearing is focused on student data privacy, I would be remiss without encouraging the committees to provide additional leadership, regulatory innovation, and investment needed to support the Nation's educational system in updating its teacher skills, infrastructure, and practices for the digital age.

I would be happy to answer any questions you might have.

Mr. MEEHAN. Thank you, Mr. MacCarthy.

The Chairman now recognizes Ms. Popp for your opening comments.

STATEMENT OF JOYCE POPP, CHIEF INFORMATION OFFICER, IDAHO STATE DEPARTMENT OF EDUCATION

Ms. POPP. Thank you, Chairman, Ranking Members, and committee Members for allowing me time to address you on the important issue of student data privacy. In education, all teachers should have access to meaningful data to support their instructional practices. We will continue our efforts, with the understanding the student-level data must be respected and protected, while also acknowledging that student information is a vital resource for teachers and school staff in their educational planning.

In Idaho, we have been working diligently to find the proper balance of strong data security policies while also supporting the stakeholders. Data stewardship has been a talking point for quite some time, teaching and encouraging school district leaders to adopt equally as strong data collecting and management policies. I have been with the Idaho State Department of Education for 5 years. My background is largely in the private sector, working in senior management for several Fortune 500 companies, dealing with information systems and information technology areas where infrastructure, e-commerce, data systems, and data security was a key focal point.

Data usage and security of information in the private sector is of the utmost importance, just as it is in the educational world. Through this experience, I have a working knowledge of data systems, and how essential it is to protect student-level data and ensure student data privacy. We live in a world where cyber threats and a chance to breach data systems are preventive, and we must make every effort to protect this data, but also to be vigilant in our data use efforts. As we all understand, however, students' data security is not the same as data privacy.

Idaho collects student-level data for reporting purposes, while also supporting State and Federal programs. We do not want to be collecting data for data's sake. However, we want to be collecting only data that is clearly needed to improve educational outcomes for the students of Idaho. We collect data at the student level, as all data must be repeatable, defensible, and auditable. All of the data elements that have been are currently being collected in Idaho have been published through our public website. We are constantly auditing and evaluating the data we collect and how we collect it to ensure that technology best practices are employed.

Through this, we have improved our efforts in supporting teachers and school administrators with quality, timely data. For years, school districts and State agencies have diligently followed the guidelines of the Family Educational Rights and Privacy Act, which provides guidance on disclosure of personally-identifiable information from educational records. Educational stakeholders and their elected officials in Idaho continue their efforts to work together in order to ensure student data is protected. This is evidenced by the crafting of our Senate Bill 1372 during the 2014 legislative session, a student data privacy bill.

The intent of Senate Bill 1372, known as the Student Data Accessibility, Transparency, and Accountability Act of 2014, is to ensure that student information is safeguarded and privacy is honored, respected, and protected, while also acknowledging that student information is a vital resource for teachers and school staff in their educational planning. The bill also includes language addressing a monetary penalty if anyone fails to protect the data and a breach of student-level data occurs or it is released without proper authorization.

Policies have also been adopted to ensure that any contractors or vendors who receive student-level data for specific purposes do not use the data outside of the specified use that is clearly called out in the contracts. All contracts, in addition to data use, are required to have specific data destruction and proof of data destruction dates. In a review of a prior contractual agreement made with vendors that were up for renewal, Idaho became aware of verbiage that stated vendors owned the data that it was provided. This verbiage is no longer allowed in any of the Idaho State Department of Education contracts.

Awareness is a key component to the adoption of this new law, and the district personnel have been notified and made aware of their responsibilities. The bill also calls for the Idaho State Board of Education to develop a model policy for school districts and public charter schools that will govern data collection, access, security, and use of such data. The model policy will be available this summer. We employee cybersecurity experts to constantly monitor and review processes and procedures, including the types of hardware and software programs purchased and deployed within our data center.

Data privacy, however, is not as easily addressed. It is everyone's responsibility. To close, Idaho has and will continue to take the proper steps in implementing data security and policies to protect the student-level data. It is our responsibility to continually strive to adapt to the constantly-changing world of technology and cyber threats. Adequate is not enough when dealing with student data privacy. We will continue to better our systems and policies to ensure that student data privacy is not just a hope in Idaho, but it is a reality.

Chairman, Ranking Members and committee Members, thank you again for this opportunity.

[The prepared statement of Ms. Popp follows:]

PREPARED STATEMENT OF JOYCE POPP

JUNE 25, 2014

Thank you Chairmen, Ranking Members, and committees Members for allowing me time to address you on the important issue of student data privacy. It is truly an honor to have this opportunity to discuss Idaho's practices around collecting and protecting student data. In education, all teachers should have access to meaningful data to support their instructional practices; data that is collected is now available to all educators, both administration and teachers in Idaho to support them in making data driven decisions to impact student achievement. We will continue our efforts with the understanding that student-level data must be respected and protected while also acknowledging that student information is a vital resource for teachers and school staff in their educational planning. In Idaho, we have been working diligently to find the proper balance of strong data security policy while also supporting stakeholders. Data stewardship has been a talking point within the Idaho State Department of Education for quite some time, teaching and encouraging school districts leaders to adopt equally as strong data collecting and management policies. This process must not only happen at the State level, but also at the school district and down to the individual teacher level.

I have been with the Idaho State Department of Education for 5 years and in the capacity of Chief Information Officer for the past several years. My background is largely in the private sector, working in Senior Management for several Fortune 500 companies, dealing in the Information Systems and Information Technology area where infrastructure, eCommerce, data systems, and data security was a key focal point. Data usage and security of information in the private sector is of the upmost of importance just as it is in the education world. Through this experience I have a working knowledge of data systems and how essential it is to protect student-level data and ensure student data privacy. All companies in the private sector secure their customer's data and likewise, State and local educational institutions must make the same or greater efforts to protect student data. We live in a world where cyber threats and attempts to breach data systems are prevalent, and we must make every effort to protect this data but also to be vigilant in our data use efforts. As we all understand however, data security is not the same as data privacy.

Idaho collects student-level data for reporting purposes while also supporting State and Federal programs. We do not want to be collecting data for data sake, however we want to be collecting only data that is clearly needed to improve educational outcomes for the students of Idaho. Currently, the State of Idaho collects attendance data for each day or portion of a day a student is in class as this is used for funding purposes and program participation; yet the State does not collect a specific reason for an absence as this is currently not a data element necessary for program or funding calculations. We collect data at the student level as all data must be repeatable, defensible, and auditable. All of the data elements that have been, and that are currently being collected have been published on the public website and made available for district personnel and patrons. Along with this information our department publishes why we collect this data, down to each individual data element. Over the past 4 years we have been receiving data from our school districts via secure measures. We are constantly auditing and evaluating the data we collect, and how we collect it to ensure that technology best practices are employed. Through this refinement process, we have improved our efforts in supporting teachers and school administrators with quality, timely data. Also in this process, we worked with our Idaho legislators and other stakeholders to create a piece of legislation that ensures that our educational institutions not only have the policies and protocols to ensure data security but also data privacy. Included in the legislation, individuals are held accountable for improper handling and use of student-level data.

For years, school districts and State agencies have diligently followed the guidelines of the Family Educational Rights and Privacy Act (FERPA) which provides guidance on disclosure of Personally Identifiable Information (PII) from educational records. Not only has Idaho followed these guidelines, but we have taken a conservative approach in the interpretation of FERPA to safeguard student-level data. Educational stakeholders and their elected officials in Idaho continue their efforts to work together in order to ensure student data is protected. This is evident by the crafting of Senate Bill 1372 during the 2014 legislative session, a student data privacy bill. Idaho utilized information and recommendations put out by the Privacy Technical Assistance Center (PTAC) through the U.S. Department of Education. As stated within the Data Governance and Stewardship document provided by PTAC, "successful data management requires a proactive approach to addressing stakeholders' needs for high-quality data, while protecting the privacy of individual respondents."

The intent of Senate Bill 1372, known as the Student Data Accessibility, Transparency, and Accountability Act of 2014, is to ensure that student information is safeguarded and that privacy is honored, respected, and protected while also acknowledging that student information is a vital resource for teachers and school staff in their educational planning. This bill also provides specific definitions and guidelines authorizing access to student data systems and to individual student data, hence our continued focus on data stewardship. The bill also includes language addressing a penalty not to exceed $50,000 if anyone within the agencies, districts, or public charters fail to protect the data and a breach of student level data occurs or is released without proper authorization. In addition to addressing use, protection and breaches of data, each public school district or charter school is required to adopt data protection and privacy policies and guidelines. Awareness is a key component to the adoption of this new law, and district personnel have been notified and made aware of this responsibility. Presentations are being conducted around the State to emphasize the details and importance of the new law.

We are also aware that not all school districts have the capacity to write data security policy; in knowing this, the bill also calls for the Idaho State Board of Education to develop a model policy for school districts and public charter schools that will govern data collection, access, security, and use of such data. The Idaho State Board of Education is currently working on the model policy and will have it available for all school districts and public charters this summer.

I have made a concerted effort to provide awareness meetings to all staff within the Idaho State Department of Education. In these meetings I discuss the intent of Senate Bill 1372, and the level of accountability, roles, and liabilities that State employees will be required to adopt as well as our obligation to educate our districts and schools of their responsibilities. Divisions within the agency handle different types of data; however an example that has been used is Child Nutrition Programs. The United States Department of Agriculture (USDA) requires a specific "need to know" basis to access free and reduced price meal eligibility information. Under the rule of the USDA, State agencies, districts, and public charters must ensure that data systems, records, and other means of accessing a student's eligibility status are limited. The "need to know" thought process is being adopted by the Idaho State Department of Education for all employees who handle or might have access to student-level data.

As Idaho has many rural and even remote school districts, we also take into consideration the population size whenever aggregating data. We have methods to mask small cell size and ensure that data is not personally identifiable even when aggregated.

Along with this thought process is also gaining the knowledge of proper transfer of student-level data. For example, we have adopted policies for data governance that prohibits student-level data being passed by email. Employees and districts have received training on encryption and other methods of data privacy and security. Sensitive information is more properly transferred using password and data encryption, through a Secure File Transfer Protocol (SFTP), again on a "need to know" basis. Policies have also been adopted to ensure that any contractors or vendors who receive student-level data for specific purposes do not use the data outside of the specified use clearly called out in the contract. All contracts, in addition to data use, are required to have specific data destruction and proof of data destruction dates. In a review of prior contractual agreements made with vendors that were up for renewal, Idaho became aware of verbiage which stated the vendor "owned" the data it was provided. This verbiage is no longer allowed on Idaho State Department of Education contracts and as previously stated we require proof of destruction and the associated dates of the destruction.

The Idaho State Department of Education receives many public records requests and researcher requests to supply student-level data. Idaho has put together policies which provide the ability to decline all such requests for student-level data. To the individual making the public records request, only aggregate data will be made available. This means data collected or reported at the group, cohort of institutional level only and will not include any Personally Identifiable Information once again taking into consideration small cell sizes within the aggregate data.

Idaho Department of Education has hired cybersecurity experts to constantly monitor and review processes and procedures, including the types of hardware and software programs purchased and deployed within our data center. Data privacy however is not as easily addressed, as it is everyone's responsibility.

To close, Idaho has and will continue to take the proper steps in implementing data security and policies to protect student-level data. It is our responsibility to continually strive to adapt to the constantly-changing world of technology and cyber threats; adequate is not enough when dealing with student data privacy. We will continue to better our systems and policies to ensure that student data privacy is not a hope in the State of Idaho, but a reality.

Chairmen, Ranking Members, and committees Members, again thank you for this opportunity and I would stand for any questions you may have.

Mr. MEEHAN. Thank you, Ms. Popp.

The Chairman now recognizes Mr. Murray for your opening comments.

STATEMENT OF THOMAS C. MURRAY, STATE AND DISTRICT DIGITAL LEARNING POLICY AND ADVOCACY DIRECTOR, ALLIANCE FOR EXCELLENT EDUCATION

Mr. MURRAY. Thank you, Mr. Chairman. I began this morning with a call from a school principal asking if I was nervous to testify in front of Congress. I said, "Sir, when you have stood in front of a thousand middle school students that are completely hormonal, that is pressure."

Thank you for having me.

Chairman Meehan, Chairman Rokita and Ranking Member Clarke, Ranking Member Loebsack and Members of the subcommittees, it is an honor to testify before you today. My goal is to illustrate how student data can be used effectively to strengthen student achievement and personalize the learning for each individual student, while simultaneously maintaining high levels of student privacy. Although I am now a State and district digital learning director at the Alliance for Excellent Education, I come to you first and foremost as an educator.

I have spent my life serving children, first as an elementary and middle school classroom teacher, then as a middle school assistant principal, an elementary principal and, most recently, as the director of technology and cyber education in the Quakertown Community School District, located in Bucks County, Pennsylvania. In each of these roles, I have balanced the use of data and its tie to student achievement, while ensuring privacy on a daily basis. Al-

31

though I could share countless stories of how data-driven decision making has forever changed the lives of students, I will take a moment to just give one example.

I knew Susan, whose name has been changed for protection, as a fourth grader. Susan had struggled tremendously in her previous school and never had much support at home. Dad left early, and Mom struggled to get by. It was evident that at home her education was never a priority. Having bounced from school to school, she had little consistency and rarely had the home support needed to be successful, always playing catch-up, with skills sometimes years behind. Life was dealing her a tough hand.

During her first few weeks in my classroom, we were able to collect a tremendous amount of data on levels of performance. For example, we looked at the various aspects of her reading, from fluency to comprehension. We found that Susan struggled with accurate and fluent word recognition, and often originates with the weaknesses in recognizing patterns of speech. It was through data collection and analysis that we were able to come to the conclusion of her exact reading needs. Based on Susan's specific needs, we were able to develop a personalized plan for success.

For example, we utilized a multifaceted approach that was digital in nature. These various software programs were overseen by, and used in connection with, dynamic instruction from her well-trained teacher. Over time, her achievement was tracked and personalized, her plan modified. Year-over-year, her performance steadily improved and she was ultimately able to cross the stage at graduation not only receiving, but truly earning, her high school diploma.

As an educator who has witnessed a myriad of stories just like Susan's, I know that her success is attributed to the data-driven personalized education that she received. There are countless students like Susan sitting in virtually every one of our Nation's classrooms. It is critical that we understand the Nation's context for today's hearing. In many ways, the effective use of data is not just an educational strategy, it is an economic strategy.

By 2018, two-thirds of the Nation's jobs will require at least some post-secondary education, and estimates indicate that the Nation will be 3 million college degrees short because too few students graduate from high school on time and prepared for post-secondary education.

Our students need and deserve an effective, world-class education to be competitive in a global economy. In the 21st Century, that means using data and technology effectively in the classroom. Just like doctors evaluate your medical history, current condition, and records from other physicians to diagnose, care, and treat patients, teachers and administrators need access to data in order to best personalize the learning for each student. Today, the alliance released a paper that I have submitted for the record describing how this is happening across the country.

In Quakertown, I was able to witness first-hand the power of data, and saw our graduation rates increase 10 percentage points over a 2-year period. Data is used at all levels to support student success. Teachers collect and analyze data on a regular basis to inform their instruction, whether it is data on reading comprehension, fluency, or math facts, teachers collect, organize, and analyze data in order to personalize instruction for each student. At the building level, I use this information as a principle to analyze trends in curriculum, strengths, and weaknesses in our academic program, and teacher effectiveness.

Tracking this data at the building level allowed me to properly allocate resources and modify schedules, from reading specialists and special ed support to a systemic response to intervention model. At the district level, our leadership team would analyze district-wide trends to make sure—make decisions about curriculum renewal, standardize assessments, professional learning, budgets, and more.

As the director of technology in Quakertown, it was my team's job to oversee the security of such data. Like other districts, we utilized the necessary firewall, security certificates, and other limitations of access to ensure that only those people with the need to know had the needed information.

For instance, only two people in the district would have access to the student information: Me, and the data specialist who would work alongside the Pennsylvania State reporting system. Teachers were only able to see information that was legally permissible for students who they taught, and they each signed a confidentiality agreement each year. We ensured compliance with SIPA as well as FERPA. For example, we utilized 128-byte encryption for instances of data transfer outside our own firewall, the same level of security used in on-line banking.

Educators across this country demonstrate every day that they know how to use this data responsibly. I offer several recommendations in my written testimony and, in closing, would like to highlight two of them. First, educators need support in how to effectively use data to improve instruction, while protecting sensitive student data. Funds from Title II of the Elementary and Secondary Education Act should be utilized for this purpose.

My second recommendation is a simple request for caution as you explore policy in this area. Privacy concerns are real. At the same time, education in the 21st Century must take advantage of all that technology has to offer. This precise sentiment was expressed yesterday in a bipartisan op-ed by two of your colleagues on the committee, Representatives Polis and Messer, in which they eloquently stated security and privacy are critical, yet manageable, concerns.

We must not dismiss the power of using data to improve classroom instruction. Simply develop best practices to ensure that data is used responsibly. We must not let fear of data prevent us from realizing the promise of technology. The Nation's students, their parents, and our economy deserve nothing less.

Thank you for the opportunity to share a school and district perspective on this important matter.

[The prepared statement of Mr. Murray follows:]

33

PREPARED STATEMENT OF THOMAS C. MURRAY

JUNE 25, 2014

INTRODUCTION

Chairman Meehan, Chairman Rokita, Ranking Member Clarke, Ranking Member Loebsack, and Members of the U.S. House of Representatives Subcommittee on Cybersecurity, Infrastructure Protection, and Security Technologies and the Subcommittee on Early Childhood, Elementary, and Secondary Education: It is an honor to testify before you today to discuss the critical role that the effective and safe use of data can play in supporting success among America's students.

My goal today is to illustrate how student data can be used effectively to strengthen student achievement and personalize the learning for each individual student while simultaneously maintaining high levels of student privacy.

Today, I come to you first and foremost as an educator. I've spent my life serving children, first as an elementary and middle school classroom teacher, then as a middle school assistant principal, an elementary principal, and most recently as the director of technology and cyber education in the rural Quakertown Community School District located in upper Bucks County, Pennsylvania. In each of these roles, I balanced the use of data and its tie to student achievement, while ensuring privacy on a daily basis.

I am now pleased to serve as the State and district digital learning director at the Alliance for Excellent Education. The Alliance is a Washington, DC-based National policy and advocacy organization dedicated to ensuring that all students, particularly those traditionally underserved, graduate from high school ready for success in college, work, and citizenship. The Alliance focuses on America's 6 million most-at-risk secondary school students—those in the lowest achievement quartile—who are most likely to leave school without a diploma or to graduate unprepared for a productive future. The Alliance's mission is to promote high school transformation to make it possible for every child to graduate prepared for success in life.

A chief part of the Alliance's mission is using technology and digital learning to provide innovative and effective ways to ensure that all students—especially those most at risk and disadvantaged—graduate from high school prepared for success.

The Alliance held the first National Digital Learning Day in 2012, an annual celebration with participation from more than 26,000 teachers and millions of students from every State in the Nation. In 2013, the Alliance announced Project 24, a new effort to assist school districts in developing a plan to use technology and high-quality digital learning, including the collection of proper and secure student learning data, to help drive new twenty-first-century student-centered instruction models leading to improved college and career readiness for all students. Currently, 1,300 school districts are participating in some way.

Although I could stand before you and share countless stories of how data-driven decision making—both in the classroom by teachers and at the district level by school administrators—has forever changed the lives of students, I'll take a moment to give just one example.

I knew Susan (name has been changed for protection) as a fourth grader. When I met her she was 9. Susan had struggled tremendously in her previous school and never had much support at home. Having bounced from school to school, she had little consistency and rarely had the home support needed to be successful. Life was dealing her a tough hand.

During her first few weeks in my classroom, we were able to collect a tremendous amount of data on her levels of performance. For example, we looked at the various aspects of her reading, from fluency to comprehension, etc. Based on Susan's exact needs, and due to the large amounts of data we were able to collect, we were able to develop a personalized plan to meet her needs. Over time, I watched as these interventions, implemented based on data-driven decisions, helped to build her confidence, and ultimately her academic skill level. As Susan moved through other data-based, personalized instructional environments, she was able close the achievement gap, and ultimately cross the stage at graduation, receiving her high school diploma. As an educator who has witnessed myriad stories like Susan, it is without a shadow of a doubt that I know that her success is attributed to her teachers and schools being able to utilize a vast amount of real-time data to develop personalized instruction to meet her needs. There are countless students just like Susan, sitting in virtually every one of our Nation's classrooms.

NEED FOR EDUCATION REFORM

In order for the United States to sustain its position as the world's leading economic power, its system of education must be rapidly and dramatically improved. By 2018, two-thirds of the Nation's jobs will require at least some post-secondary education, and estimates indicate that the Nation will be 3 million college degrees short.[1] Approximately 30 percent of African American and Hispanic students do not graduate on time, if at all,[2] and 20 percent of students who do make it to college need at least one remedial course,[3] meaning that they are paying college prices for the high school education they should have already received.

This poor preparation is taking place at a time when the economic demand for a highly educated workforce has never been greater. Over the past 40 years, the percentage of jobs requiring post-secondary education has doubled (from 28 percent to 59 percent).[4] The demands of the knowledge-driven economy are far outpacing the production of students who are prepared for the workforce. To respond to this rapidly rising demand for a higher-skilled workforce, every State has raised its academic standards to require that every student graduate from high school ready for college and a career.

While States are working to strengthen education in order to meet the demand for a highly-educated workforce, the Nation's demographics are rapidly changing. Students of color make up more than half of the K–12 population in 12 States and comprise between 40 and 50 percent of the student population in an additional 10 States.[5] The Nation's fastest-growing student populations are those that the traditional education system is least equipped to serve.

This seismic tremor in education means that the Nation must provide a higher-quality educational experience to more students than it ever has before. Only the effective use of data and technology supporting teachers will accomplish this major objective.

EFFECTIVE USE OF DATA IS CRITICAL TO EDUCATION REFORM

Data can be a powerful tool for personalizing learning for each student and increasing achievement in the highest-need schools. Just like doctors evaluate your medical history, current condition, and records from other physicians to diagnose, care, and treat patients, teachers, and administrators need access to data in order to best personalize learning for each student, for they too are assessing, diagnosing, and treating the various needs of our Nation's students.

Today, the Alliance released a paper—*Capacity Enablers and Barriers for Learning Analytics: Implications for Policy and Practice*—that describes how learning analytics initiatives are helping States and districts move from being data collectors to data analyzers.[6] The full paper is included in my complete testimony submitted for the record. Learning analytics applies techniques from science, sociology, psychology, and statistics to analyze student information. It enables the effective use of data to improve instruction in meaningful ways, such as those that adapt instructional content, intervene with at-risk students, and provide feedback.

When student data is collected properly and used effectively, it can be an integral part of personalizing instruction to improve learning. Data can guide digital learning to target instruction. It can provide real-time feedback on student progress that allows teachers to tailor instruction, resources, and time.

Throughout my time in Quakertown, I was able to witness this first-hand. As the district implemented a personalized approach to instruction, with decisions predicated on data-driven decision making, we were able to create an environment where student learning and growth was at the forefront. Through this technology-infused, data-driven environment, we saw high school graduation rates increase 10 percent-

[1] A. Carnevale, N. Smith, J. Strohl, *Help Wanted: Projections of Jobs and Education Requirements Through 2018* (Washington, DC: Georgetown University Center on Education and the Workforce, 2010).

[2] R. Stillwell and J. Sabel: *Public High School Four-Year On-Time Graduation Rates and Event Dropout Rates: School Years 2010–11 and 2011–12* (First Look) (NCES 2014–391) (Washington, DC: U.S. Department of Education, National Center for Education Statistics, 2014).

[3] D. Sparks and N. Malkus, *Statistics in Brief: First-Year Undergraduate Remedial Coursetaking: 1999–2000, 2003–04, 2007–08* (NCES 2013–013) (Washington, DC: U.S. Department of Education, National Center for Education Statistics, 2013), *http://nces.ed.gov/pubs2013/2013013.pdf* (accessed February 11, 2014).

[4] A. Carnevale et al., *Help Wanted*.

[5] W. DeBaun, *Inseparable Imperatives: Equity in Education and the Future of the American Economy* (Washington, DC: Alliance for Excellent Education, 2012).

[6] M.A. Wolf, R. Jones, R. Wise, *Capacity Enablers and Barriers for Learning Analytics: Implications for Policy and Practice* (Washington, DC: Alliance for Excellent Education, 2014).

age points over a 2-year period. Upon my recent departure from the district, we had more students taking rigorous courses than ever before, the State standardized test scores were the highest they've ever been, and results on tests such as the SAT showed significant growth over time.

Our Nation, schools, and leaders must be careful not to let fear of data thwart progress toward the best learning strategies for all students. At the same time, teachers, principals, and district and State leaders must be mindful and purposeful about the appropriate collection and use of data. Overly restricting data because of the fears of some will be devastating to modern, innovative teaching practices. There must be support for policies that effectively address privacy, safety, and security concerns related to digital learning and other ways that data is stored including antiquated paper file storage. In doing so, it is important to differentiate between real and perceived threats so that we can take advantage of the real potential to improve learning outcomes for students through the proper use of data.

Pulling from my 14 years of school district service, I'd like to share a few examples of how the use of data transforms and personalizes instruction for students and how school districts use data to systemically plan and problem solve to meet the needs of their student population.

Having been a classroom teacher for 6 years, and supervising classrooms for 5 years as a principal thereafter, data played and continues to play a vital role in the daily instructional process. Teachers collect and analyze data on a regular basis to inform their instruction. Whether it's specific data regarding reading levels, comprehension, fluency, math facts, or information surrounding a specific academic standard, teachers collect, organize, and analyze data in order to personalize instruction for each student. Without such collection, teachers would lose the ability to pinpoint the exact needs of each child and would lose the ability to treat each need with precision. Best practices indicate that meeting each student where they are will push them to their highest levels of achievement. But this is only feasible through personalized learning and instruction, which can only occur when up-to-date data is readily available so that teachers can make real-time instructional decisions, allowing them to put their students' needs at the heart of teaching and learning.

At the building level—and as both a middle school and elementary principal—this data was used to analyze grade levels, trends in curriculum, strengths, and weaknesses in our academic program, and grade level and teacher effectiveness. Tracking this data on a large scale at the building level allowed me to properly allocate resources, from reading specialists and special education support, to a systemic response to intervention model. On a weekly basis, Quakertown's teacher and specialists would meet in data teams to discuss every child and what we could do better or differently to meet their individual needs—both for those needing additional support and those who needed high levels of enrichment. We would then use this information to design schedules for support and intervention for all students, both at the classroom and building levels.

As I moved to Quakertown's district office, the ability to collect, analyze, and dissect student data on a large scale was even more important. At the highest levels, our leadership team would analyze district-wide trends, which allowed us to identify and plan for needs moving forward. These areas of need would help us formulate district goals, and over the long term, strategic plans. Without objective academic data on the large scale, the ability to make district-wide decisions about curriculum renewal, standardized assessments, professional learning, budget, etc. would be jeopardized.

As it relates to special education, very specific achievement data would be used to build an Individualized Education Program (IEP) for each child, as required under the Individuals with Disabilities Education Act. These goals would then be measured throughout the course of each year and revised on a year-over-year basis to chart growth and achievement and ensure that our Nation's students with disabilities receive both what they need and deserve.

As both a principal and cabinet-level member at the district office, part of my role was to ensure high-quality teaching in the classroom, which was monitored through the teacher supervision process. As such, supervisors had access to student data and were able to longitudinally track performance of teacher effectiveness over time. In order to prepare students for their tomorrow, there must be high-quality teachers in the classroom today; and being able to objectively assess effectiveness, over time, is imperative.

As the director of technology at Quakertown, it was my team's job to oversee the security of such data, including data stored in our data warehouse and student information system. Like other districts, we utilized the necessary firewalls, security certificates, and limitations on access to ensure that only those people with a need to know had the needed information. For instance, only two people in the district would have access to all student information; me and the data specialist who would work on the district's Pennsylvania State Reporting System. Teachers were only able to see information that was legally permissible for students who they taught, and principals and specialists would be granted access to their building-level data. This information was treated with the highest levels of security and accountability, even going as far as having every staff member sign a confidentiality agreement, every year, which clearly delineates the expectations of how they were to handle the student data to which they had access.

On the educational technology front, the Quakertown district would partner with various companies on tools and resources from on-line registration, ranging from our student information system and gradebook to various assessment and testing tools. For each company, we'd work to ensure compliance with the Family Educational Rights and Privacy Act (FERPA), and with instances of data transfer—such as that of on-line registration—there was a 128-bit encryption in place, the same level of security used in on-line banking. When it came to various web tools, we'd work to ensure compliance with the Children's Internet Protection Act, paying special attention and giving extra precautions to those students under 13 years of age. It was the district's legal obligation to ensure that the highest levels of security for this data were in place, and something that was always at the top of our priority list.

OTHER EXAMPLES OF SUCCESS

In my role at the Alliance, I have seen States and districts across the country using data effectively. In Kentucky, for example, K–12 and post-secondary data is linked in order to provide feedback reports to high schools on matters such as college readiness and ACT scores. This data can be used to reduce the large number of students who need remediation when they leave high school. In Oregon, professional development on instructional strategies is paired with technical training so that educators can use data regularly to improve instruction.

A particularly powerful example of the effective use of data comes from Chicago Public Schools (CPS), the Nation's third-largest school district. In 2007, CPS initiated a reform to utilize data in order to prevent students from dropping out. Evidence shows that students who end their 9th-grade year on track to graduation are almost 4 times more likely to graduate from high school than those who are off-track. Therefore, CPS promoted the use of data to monitor students' performance, help teachers intervene before students fell too far behind, and implement a variety of interventions to address the specific needs facing students as identified by the data. At the center of this effort were monthly data reports given to each high school that allowed educators to respond when students were heading in the wrong direction.

As a result of this effort to effectively use data to keep students in school, the percentage of 9th-grade students who are on-track to graduation has risen 25 points, from 57 to 82 percent, and graduation rates have increased 13 percentage points.[7]

RECOMMENDATIONS

Whether in rural Quakertown, or urban Chicago, the power of data to improve student achievement is real. Data can and must be used responsibly, and educators across the country demonstrate every day that they are able to effectively use student data while maintaining student privacy. On behalf of the Alliance for Excellent Education, I offer recommendations for your consideration in order to improve the ability of our Nation's teachers and schools to use data to strengthen student achievement.

(1) *Professional development.*—Educators need support in how to effectively use data to improve instruction while protecting sensitive student data. Funds from Title II of the Elementary and Secondary Education Act should be utilized for this purpose.

(2) *Early warning indicator and intervention systems.*—Schools and districts across the country are implementing early warning indicator and intervention systems in order to identify struggling students and provide support that is tailored to their individual needs. There are many ways in which Federal policy

[7] M. Roderick, T. Kelley-Kemple, D. Johnson, and N. Beechum, *Preventable Failure: Improvements in Long-Term Outcomes When High Schools Focused on Ninth Grade Year: Research Summary* (Chicago: University of Chicago Consortium on Chicago School Research, 2014), https://ccsr.uchicago.edu/sites/default/files/publications/On-Track%20Validation%20RS.pdf (accessed June 23, 2014).

can support the implementation of early warning indicator and intervention systems, including requiring them as a component of Federal School Improvement Grant program.

(3) Data transparency.—Parents and the public must know what data is being used to support students, and they must be given access to this information.

- It is imperative that the public, and parents in particular, know what student data is being collected and why. States and school districts should each provide readily and publicly accessible information on the types of individual student data they maintain and how it is collected and used, who has access to protected data, and what safeguards are in place to protect it. School districts must ensure that their individual schools are meeting the district requirements.

- The Family Educational Rights and Privacy Act, or FERPA, currently gives parents and eligible students aged 18 or older access to their education records. Following the example set in health care through the Health Insurance Portability and Accountability Act, or HIPAA, access should be expanded so that data is also available for parents and eligible students in an electronic and cost-efficient format. School districts should explore creating encrypted and password-protected websites to make this information readily accessible to parents and eligible students in a safe and protected manner while protecting it from exposure to unauthorized individuals.

(4) Data protection.—Strong policies and plans are vital in data collection to safeguard privacy. States, districts, and schools must have a data protection infrastructure to ensure that personally identifiable student data is protected. States should designate a chief privacy officer who is responsible and held accountable for the implementation of sound privacy policy. Duties would include monitoring data collection practices, insuring compliance with Federal and State laws, overseeing a data security compliance plan and emergency data breach response plan, and tracking the latest technological improvements and best practices in data collection and privacy. Districts should designate a single point of contact who focuses on privacy issues. Some districts may consider exploring whether they should designate a district chief privacy officer depending on their size, individual needs, and cost feasibility of implementation.

(5) Policy for learning in the 21st Century.—Privacy protection policies must be updated and modernized to ensure student privacy is protected. Simultaneously, legislative bodies must be cautious to avoid creating policies that hinder learning. Education in the 21st Century must take advantage of all that technology has to offer, recognizing that learning takes place in and outside of the classroom. To this end, the bipartisan Aspen Institute Task Force on Learning and the Internet recently issued the report Learning at the Center of a Networked World, which offers recommendations for policymakers at all levels for consideration and action.[8]

CONCLUSION

There is a difference between rhetoric and reality. Privacy concerns are real, and school leaders and policy makers must continue to deal with these very real concerns systemically and transparently. At the same time, it is imperative that this policy debate serves as a mechanism for spurring innovation, rather than stifling it. The U.S. Congress and State legislative bodies should explore modernizing privacy protection through proactive laws that encourage data use while protecting it to better reflect today's world, thus avoiding sudden reactionary policies that create unnecessary and undue constraints on learning. The Nation's students, their parents, and its economy deserve nothing less.

Mr. MEEHAN. Thank you, Mr. Murray. I thank all of our panelists for their opening comments. and before I recognize myself for questions, I would like to ask unanimous consent to enter in the record the Fordham Law School report on privacy and cloud computing in public schools, authored by Mr. Joel Reidenberg.

Mr. MEEHAN. Without objection, so ordered.*

---

[8] Aspen Institute Task Force on Learning and the Internet, *Learning at the Center of a Networked World* (Washington, DC: Author, 2014), *http://aspeninstitute.fsmdev.com/documents/AspenReportFinalPagesRev.pdf* (accessed June 23, 2014).

*The information has been retained in committee files.

Mr. MEEHAN. I now recognize myself for opening questions. Mr. Reidenberg, let me begin with you. I think we all appreciate the points so eloquently made by Mr. Murray in his commentary about the opportunities for individualized education that can now be realized by virtue of technology. Nobody wants to try to inhibit that personalized development. But I brought with me here the perspective of us dealing with issues like the NSA, and simple concern on the part of American people because the Government was aware of who you called, what telephone number was called by another telephone number.

As I began to look at this issue, I appreciated that the courts themselves have determined things like homework assignments or other kinds of in-class work which is now available for exactly that personalized information. Every keystroke may be being recorded. So you are learning a vast amount about that student's analysis and ability to deal with an issue. But we are also gathering that forever. The concern is that that information, you are seeing 95 percent of it. Or big percentages of it are no longer being held within the school itself, oftentimes going off somewhere in the cloud and becoming the property of third-party vendors.

This is where the rubber meets the road for me, in my concern about this issue. How much not just private information, but like a health care record. There is some party—third-party vendor, I don't even know who it is—they know a lot more about my child than I know. Worse yet, is there the possibility that information lives otherwise? So a point that was made by one of the panelists that identifies a learning disability or difficulty that somebody may have. Suppose that information continues and gets purchased or sold by the very same company that many want to hire somebody some day.

So where are the gaps and where are the limitations on the utilization of this very personal, private information that gets moved into a public sector ownership? Then how do we contain it so that it doesn't get abused?

Mr. REIDENBERG. Mr. Chairman, I think you have put your finger on the precise problem that we are facing today. It isn't just the parents who don't know where the information is, it is also the schools. In our research, the irony of that 95 percent statistic, we know that the school that reported they didn't outsource to the cloud actually does. We learned that after we completed the students. So if we take a school districts that responded, it turns out it is, in fact, 100 percent, not 95. We found, in asking school districts what they were doing in calls to school districts, it was very difficult to find anyone on the staff who even knew what kinds of outsourcing arrangements they had.

When we look at how FERPA applies to this, FERPA is a funding statute. FERPA conditions the receipt of Federal funds by educational agencies to those agencies adhering—it is essentially confidentiality. It exempts out, though, a substantial amount of information, directory information, which includes a student's age, height, weight. It is exempted, it is not covered by the confidentiality unless the families opt out. So it is a very complex statute. But it was designed essentially as a hook on Federal financing.

It doesn't apply directly to any of these third parties. The third parties can get data from school districts under, in this context, the school official exception, which is an exception essentially written into the statute by the Department of Education. It is not spelled out, in fact, in the statute. It is not challengeable. The court challenges to recent Department of Education regulations were thrown out on standing issues. Families who feel that they have been aggrieved have no remedies because the Supreme Court has ruled there are no private rights of action in the context of FERPA.

The Department of Education, in the 40-year history, has never issued any sanction to a school district for violating FERPA. So if you look at the statute itself, even for what it covers it has some shortcomings that are quite significant. But in this context, what is so hard is that the kinds of outsourcing that take place are so complex that it is very difficult, as you pointed out in your question—it is very difficult to figure out exactly what is going on with this use of information and where to put the control.

I don't think it is the vendors' own data in a true property sense. What we find is, it is transferred pursuant to some sort of contract. That contract can spell out what the vendors' usage rights are. We don't see those contracts actually spelling out that the district truly controls the data, their kids' data. There are school districts all across the country, so there could be multiple different forms of contracts all across the country. Well, you touched an awful lot.

My time has expired. I know we will get into it. Mr. MacCarthy, I will ask it, I hope, in the context if we do not get a chance for you to speak to some of those very same issues, then I will come back to you and ask you some of those questions. But I think my colleagues will get to a lot of that as we move forward.

So at this point in time, I turn it over to Ranking Member for her questioning. Thank you.

Ms. CLARKE. Thank you, Mr. Chairman. I thank our panelists for lending their expertise to this very important subject matter today.

One of the issues that sort of dawned on me as I heard you discuss this was just the level of complexity and the myriad of circumstances under which data breaches actually occur. There are a whole host of bad actors out there seizing opportunities to assume identifies through identity theft. It just begs the question as to whether you have observed sort-of systemic protocols that are in place for reporting data breaches. Most companies, you know, they are looking to assert their brand as the best brand. It is somewhat, you know, scary for them and their bottom line to have to admit any vulnerability within their systems, the systems that they are trying to sell that they have multiple customers for.

Have any of you raised that question or encountered the type of protocols that would alert the users from the school systems themselves to be actual subjects of the usage of data breaches? I would be interested in that.

Mr. REIDENBERG. We found that almost no contracts required vendors to tell the school districts if there has been a breach. The State breach notification laws might apply, but there is wide variety of the scope of those breach notification rules. We found that notifications of parents of the existence of these third-party on-line services being used by the school districts was quite rare. So we saw no indication of any district informing its parents that there had been a breach.

Ms. CLARKE. Parents trust schools to safeguard their children's confidential and sensitive data. Can you tell us how education officials should be seeking ways to protect students' personal identifiable information? What are the contractual pressures that exist when school systems hire, or use tools from, for-profit companies to manage their students data?

Mr. REIDENBERG. So there are a variety of basic security practices that the school districts certainly need to be engaging in. If they are transferring data it has to be encrypted. They should be minimizing the identifying data. They shouldn't be using Social Security numbers, for example, that some districts around the country still do. Their contracts need to have stringent security requirements on their outside vendors. That is nonexistent right now. We saw an appalling number of districts that—vendor contracts that did not include obligations to secure the data.

It is not to say that the vendors are treating the data with abandon. We don't know. What we do know is that there is no legal protection that is being imposed on the vendors through the contracts.

Ms. CLARKE. The other element of vulnerability within systems is the age of the system. I would wonder whether, in your experience—particularly in school districts that are not as wealthy—whether the systems they are using to transmit data, you know, have reached their shelf life, if you will, in terms of vulnerabilities. What challenge that can place.

Mr. REIDENBERG. I think that is quite likely. I mean, the kinds of school districts, the sizes of the school districts across the country will range from the large cities that may have a million students in the district to places that have 300. The district that has 300 students in it, if it is using a well-designed cloud service that is gonna be more secure than the district's own IT system, most likely. So there is an advantage to using professional hosting services that a district couldn't do. The downside is, if that hosting service is now hosting data on 20 million students it becomes a honey pot for cyber attackers.

Ms. CLARKE. Very well.

Mr. Chairman, I yield back the balance of my time. Thank you.

Mr. MEEHAN. I thank the Ranking Member.

The Chairman now turns to the Chairman of the Education Committee, Mr. Rokita.

Mr. ROKITA. I thank the Chairman. I also thank the Ranking Members. Excellent testimony from everyone. I have really learned a lot, and will continue to learn as this issue goes forward.

Ms. Popp, I would like to start with you. I am always encouraged, as a former State-wide elected official, when we have solutions that come from the States. Now that is how this was set up, and I am particularly pleased with your testimony. To make sure I understood it right, are you saying that the 1372, or whatever number it was, prescribes contractual terms that have to be used when districts contract? Or by virtue of the statute alone, it is saying what is prohibited and what is allowed under district's usual procedures?

Ms. POPP. Thank you, Chairman. Senate Bill 13——

41

Mr. MEEHAN. Ms. Popp, I am gonna ask if you speak into the microphone and make sure that you push the button.

Ms. POPP. Yes, the red button is on.

Mr. MEEHAN. Okay, great. Thanks.

Ms. POPP. Thank you. Senate Bill 1372 was very clearly outlined what data and how data can be collected. It also addresses the fact that there is a monetary penalty for any breaches. It does not get into some of the very specifics on some of the policies that the Department of Education, however, has adopted. One of the things being the contractual component. It does, in the Senate bill address some of the information on contracts with third-party vendors, such as testing the agencies and student information. It actually calls out those two particular vendors directly in the Senate bill.

Mr. ROKITA. Thank you very much.

Mr. MacCarthy, what do you think of Idaho's approach? What would your members think?

Mr. MACCARTHY. Thank you for your question, Mr. Chairman. We like the approach.

Mr. ROKITA. Good.

Mr. MACCARTHY. I think it sets up the proper sort of framework for the inclusion of the appropriate issues within school contracts. As many of you have heard in previous testimony, transparency is a key element. We need to tell parents what information is being collected by the school and school vendors, what is done with it, who it is transferred to, who it is shared with, what the data security requirements are, what the data breach notification requirements are. That information should all be provided to parents, and model policies at the State level that—make sure that those issues are covered in contracts are something that the industry would support. They are part of the SIAA best practices that we put out in February of this year. So we would encourage that level of involvement by State and local and school districts.

Mr. ROKITA. Thank you.

Mr. Reidenberg, what do you think of Idaho's approach?

Mr. REIDENBERG. I think it is very encouraging. I think it is very encouraging, Mr. Chairman. I also think it is extremely positive that the Department—I know Department of Education is spelling out what the contracting practices need to be for the districts. I do think that, though, that kind of approach needs to be seen on a Nation-wide basis and that it is not just the students of Idaho that deserve the kinds of protections that Idaho is enacting.

The Federal Government is funding, in the last couple of years, anywhere between—it is probably between $500 million and a billion dollars to the States to encourage and be developing these kinds of information systems. I think we need to see approaches like that more systemically deployed across the country.

Mr. ROKITA. Do you think Mr. Murray has a good idea when he says Title II funds ought to be used in this area? Title II funds——

Mr. REIDENBERG. I am sorry.

Mr. ROKITA [continuing]. As your PRAP in those kinds of things. In fact, the Student Success Act that our whole committee passed and that sits on Mr. Reid's desk right now—block grants, a lot of Title II funds to the State so that they could use these funds in the best way they see fit. Wouldn't you say States should be able to use Federal money to help protect, or enforce, issues in this area?

Mr. REIDENBERG. Well, I think—I mean, I think that if the Federal Government is going to be financing these kinds of programs at the State level that require the generation and collection of lots of student information, then there ought to be a commensurate requirement that the States address privacy as part of their infrastructure development. When the teacher said I am not very familiar with Title II, to the extent that it is involving, say, teacher training programs, that is a key part——

Mr. ROKITA. Sir, I am afraid my time has run out. Two short questions—two short remaining questions, yes or no. Do you know of any legal malpractice cases occurring in the United States that involve attorneys for school districts or schools in this area for their lack of preparing a contract correctly or anything like that?

Mr. REIDENBERG. I am not aware of any.

Mr. ROKITA. Are you aware of any school district in this country that doesn't have legal counsel?

Mr. REIDENBERG. Yes.

Mr. ROKITA. What percentage of the total would you think that is?

Mr. REIDENBERG. That, I couldn't tell you. I mean, we saw school districts, the smaller school districts seemed to be winging it when they come to these sorts of contracts.

Mr. ROKITA. Mr. Chairman, I thank you for the time.

Mr. MEEHAN. I thank the Chairman.

I now recognize the Ranking Member, Mr. Loebsack, for his questions.

Mr. LOEBSACK. Thank you, Mr. Chairman. Before I begin my questions, I would request unanimous consent to submit two written statements if I might. One from my colleague, our colleague, Representative Jared Polis and another from Aimee Guidera. She is the executive of Data Quality Campaign.

Mr. MEEHAN. Without objection, so ordered.*

[The information follows:]

STATEMENT OF AIMEE ROGSTAD GUIDERA, EXECUTIVE DIRECTOR, DATA QUALITY CAMPAIGN

JUNE 25, 2014

Thank you for the opportunity to offer written testimony today on such an important topic for all of us in this country. The conversations parents, educators, and others are having in communities around the Nation about the use of data in education and the critical need to ensure the safeguarding of student data are important ones, and they will lead to solutions that assure all of us student data are being used safely by those we entrust with the responsibility of using them to improve student achievement. This conversation about data privacy and security is not unique to education: As a society, we are dealing with the unprecedented need to adapt to the increasing role of data in helping us make better-informed decisions and attain better services and outcomes in every aspect of our lives. Integral to this is a need to also discuss how we safeguard data and protect our personal privacy.

The Data Quality Campaign, a nonpartisan, nonprofit advocacy organization, works with policymakers and other stakeholders to highlight the power of effective data use at all levels to support families and educators in their efforts to improve student achievement.

---

*The testimony of Hon. Polis has been previously included.

This hearing provides an excellent public forum for having these vital discussions about the value, use, and protection of data. Thank you for allowing the Data Quality Campaign to submit written testimony.

USING DATA EFFECTIVELY CAN IMPROVE EDUCATION DECISION MAKING AND OUTCOMES

Like every other sector focused on getting better results, education is using data in new and game-changing ways. We are using data to inform decision making in education and improve outcomes to the level that every parent expects, every child deserves, and the future health and well-being of this Nation requires. Because of the investment the Federal, State, and local governments have made in increasing the quality, availability and use of education data, teachers and parents have better access to information that helps them tailor learning to the needs of each student in real time, and more students are walking across the graduation stage prepared for post-secondary education and the workforce. At the same time, Americans are raising legitimate questions about how we safeguard data while using them for this important purpose.

Empowered with the right data, teachers can better track their students' progress and tailor teaching to each child's needs, and parents can have a more substantive, timely account of how their kids are doing.

When education stakeholders are using data to inform their judgment at all levels, student achievement grows. States' efforts to support the effective use of data have yielded many positive developments. Parents, educators, and policymakers in Kentucky can now review high school feedback reports to get a richer picture of how well-prepared graduates from a specific high school are for college-level work, and then make changes in policy and practice to better align high school course-taking and graduation requirements with post-secondary expectations. Data coaches in Delaware can help teachers pinpoint what interventions students need most. And an early warning system in Massachusetts gives educators information that, when acted upon in a timely manner, can mean the difference between a student graduating or dropping out.

To fully leverage data to inform decisions and improve outcomes, its collection and uses must be aligned to the needs of teachers, parents, students, and policymakers. Equally important, the privacy, security, and confidentiality of the data must be safeguarded. People will not use data that they do not find useful and trustworthy. There can be no effective data use without building trust that the data will help and that it will be kept safe and secure.

All of us in education must do more to make sure that we are transparent—especially with parents about what data are collected, who has access to them, how they are used, and what policies and practices are in place to protect privacy and keep the data secure.

ALL EDUCATION DATA REQUIRE PROTECTION

Part of the rising concerns around the security, and privacy of education data stems from the need to better clarify how current laws apply to the different types of data collected; this includes if and when data may be used commercial purposes and what limits are placed on access to students' Personally Identifiable Information.

The Family Education Rights and Privacy Act (FERPA) defines the types of data that are collected in an education record (Authority: 20 U.S.C. 1232g[a][4]) as those that are "maintained by an educational agency or institution or by a party acting for the agency or institution." This includes both the information traditionally collected by an education agency like grades, test scores, gender, age, and attendance, as well as information collected by a third-party service provider which has been contracted by the education agency to provide explicit educational services.

Privacy and legal experts continue to debate whether or not data that is collected and maintained by third-party software providers, and not on behalf of an education agency is governed by FERPA. These third-party solutions provide learning apps and other technology and web-based services to inform and improve student learning. The data collected directly from a user (generally a student or parent) through these services are collected and maintained by the company providing the service and not at the request of an educational agency.

Some of these services not governed under FERPA, (for children 13 and under), however, are covered in the latest guide for businesses, parents, and small entities regarding the *Children's On-line Privacy Protection Act (COPPA)* released by the Federal Trade Commission this spring.

Because these data are collected for different purposes and involve different parties, it is necessary to create policies addressing specific concerns and ensure that data are used and maintained in a secure and effective manner. The concerns currently being raised by parents and other education stakeholders are legitimate and must be addressed in policy and practice to build understanding of their purpose and trust in their protection.

STATE ACTIONS TO SAFEGUARD STUDENT DATA

In response to these tremendous opportunities and advancements in the uses of data, many States and education agencies are also thinking about the governance and privacy responsibilities associated with data use. To support these efforts, Education Counsel released *Key Elements for Strengthening State Laws and Policies Pertaining to Student Data Use, Privacy, and Security: Guidance for State Policymakers.* The report, which highlights relevant Federal laws, State practices, and emerging best practices, serves as a helpful guide for policymakers at the Federal, State, and local levels seeking to ensure policies include foundational elements:

1. Statement of the purposes of the State's privacy policies, including an acknowledgment of the educational value of data and the importance of privacy and security safeguards.
2. Selection of a State leader and advisory board responsible for ensuring appropriate privacy and security protections, including for developing and implementing policies and for providing guidance and sharing best practices with schools and districts.
3. Establishment of a public data inventory and an understandable description of the specific data elements included in the inventory.
4. Strategies for promoting transparency and public knowledge about data use, storage, retention, destruction, and protections.
5. Development of State-wide policies for governing Personally Identifiable Information.
6. Establishment of a State-wide data security plan to address administrative, physical, and technical safeguards.

Since January 2014, 36 State legislatures have introduced 108 bills directed at ensuring the privacy, security, and confidentiality of education data. Many of these States recognize that FERPA is a strong foundation for student privacy, but that they should tailor additional laws to address the specific concerns of their citizens.

Several States have passed legislation this session to proactively and publicly ensure that education data are used effectively and ethically. Colorado's recently passed H.B. 1294 provides definitions of key data terms and describes permissible uses of education data. The law also requires the provision of supports needed to ensure the privacy and transparency of the State's education data use, including a public data inventory, data privacy training for Department staff, breach notification processes, and contracting guidelines for working with service providers. In addition to describing when data can be shared and calling for new privacy and security policies, West Virginia H.B. 4316 delineates State, district, and school responsibilities in creating and maintaining a student data inventory; the law also provides for a data governance officer and describes his or her responsibilities.

Some new State laws seek to establish stronger mechanisms for determining how student data will be used through the creation of data governance bodies with decision making or investigatory authority. Indiana's H.B. 1003 establishes the Indiana Network of Knowledge (INK), a group charged with data governance and making the State's data transparent and accessible to the public. Maine L.D. 1194 creates a Joint Standing Committee on Judiciary to study student privacy (especially with regard to social media and cloud computing services), concerns of parents about online education data service providers using data to build student profiles or target on-line advertising, and how other States address student privacy with social media and cloud computing services. South Carolina H.B. 3893 describes permissible State data collections and calls for security and access rules, but it also provides for the implementation of a Data Governance Committee to make decisions about data disclosures.

While most of the student data privacy bills introduced this session have focused on the student data collected by districts, some bills have begun to address data collected through the use of on-line programs and services, such as content programs and classroom apps, which fall into the category of data collected by service providers. A currently active bill in California (S.B. 1177) is one of the few bills which seek to explicitly govern data collected through education technology providers. The bill would prohibit on-line K–12 service providers from selling student data or from using, sharing, or disclosing certain types of student data for any purpose other than the contracted purpose or for "maintaining, developing, and improving the integrity and effectiveness of the site, service, or application." Other bills, such as

45

Idaho S.B. 1372, Massachusetts H.B. 331, and Tennessee H.B. 1549/S.B. 1835, prohibit the collection or use of student data for commercial purposes. The Tennessee bills, which have been signed into law, also prohibit the collection of student data for product development.

CONCLUSION

While the above examples highlight the work that States and others have done to protect the privacy and security of education data and promote data being used effectively to improve student achievement, it is important to note that this is only part of the work the field must undertake to address the concerns around education data collected by service providers. This hearing and others like it at the Federal and State levels will raise awareness of the need to address public concerns about the use of data in education.

It is important for privacy and legal experts to continue to debate the solutions as we continue to gather information. Equally important, Congress should continue to lead these discussions among all stakeholders to review existing laws including how they apply to the use of continuously changing technology to collect data and determine what gaps may exist and if necessary, how they should be addressed through new laws. Efforts like the one led by Congressmen Jared Polis (D, CO–2) and Luke Messer (R, IN–6) to encourage leaders in the education service provider field to develop standards of conduct are a promising start, and can lead to further conversations.

In addition to clarifying how existing law protects data and how it can be strengthened, there are many actions that the sector must prioritize: Building the understanding of the need for every school, district, State, and vendor to prioritize the safeguarding of education data; increasing capacity of the field through training around data security and privacy; increasing tailored communications around the value, use, and protection of data with parents and citizens; adapting emerging best practices from other sectors; and creating standards of conduct for the field to use.

It is important that these conversations, like this Congressional hearing, are not just about the "risks" of using data in education. We must all help the American public better understand the promising uses of this data to improve the performance of our schools and to ensure that every child in this country graduates prepared for success in post-secondary education and the workforce.

Mr. LOEBSACK. Thank you, Mr. Chairman. Thank you. This is an exciting time in education, there is no question. Students and teachers really have never before had so much information at their fingertips. You know, we can all recognize clearly that, through the internet, students have access to a world of multimedia educational resources. With the use of data, teachers and school leaders today have a clearer sense, I think, of individual strengths and needs of each of their students.

I want to step back just a moment from sort-of what we have been talking about up to this point. We all recognize, you know, what the problem is, potentially, out there and we have got to do something about it. But if I could ask Mr. Murray just to sort-of give us a sense—you already did a little bit. But, you know, because I am concerned about throwing the baby out with the bath water, if you will. But what can be done today with data to support student learning that couldn't be done 20 years ago, for example?

Mr. MURRAY. Sure, and that is a great question. I appreciate you asking that. The classroom has changed dramatically in the past 20 years. When I think back 20 years ago, I think back to a one-size-fits-all approach. All students were reading the same thing. If you were high up, you helped the kids that were struggling. If you were struggling, you kind of tried to get by. Teachers might offer students—and they may, at the end of a quarter, say your child earned a B because the average was an 86 percent because here is the average of everything that your kid did over the marking period.

Fast forward 20 years and look at a parent conference. When I am a parent, and I can hear very specific standards or very specific information about what my child needs—not just that it is an 86 percent overall—and get that very specific concrete information there is incredible opportunity in communication and transparency for parents, based on what their child needs. Parents are incredible stakeholders in this process. They—we, as school districts, need to be transparent and need to be able to share very specific information on student growth.

Let me give you another example. Much of our data is available on-line to our students through very secure parent portals that they create their own user name and passwords for. So no longer is it, at the end of a marking period, you get a report card and, as a parent, you only get to see that four times a year. Our parents from where I came from, they got a daily report card. They could log in to a secure system, see attendance rates, see quizzes, see anything that was up-to-date at a point in time, at that moment in time.

What does that do? That helps our children be successful. In a classroom—one last example—if I am a teacher with access to real-time data I can make decisions on the fly in the classroom. It is no longer about planning a one-size-fits-all lesson. It is about looking at data through the use of technology inside the classroom to make decisions on the fly for my kids. A quick example of that would be I am giving a lesson, I am able to electronically receive feedback exactly for every child, every answer, every time, no longer just the kid in the back of the classroom with his hand up. Make decisions as a teacher, on the fly, as what to do next right there in the classroom. Twenty years ago, that was not feasible.

Mr. LOEBSACK. Thank you, Mr. Murray. By the way, your comment about facing a thousand middle school students? That is a lot worse than facing us.

[Laughter.]

Mr. LOEBSACK. As somebody who is out of the college level for 24 years, my wife taught second grade. I understand where you are coming from. Given your teaching background and your administrative background, I think you have kind-of a unique perspective on all this. You mentioned some recommendations, couple recommendations. Practically speaking, we have to try to figure out a balance, if you will, between effectively using data to improve instruction, and ensuring the privacy protections that we are all concerned about. Can you elaborate not only on the two, but maybe some others that you have in mind?

Mr. MURRAY. Sure, absolutely. To me, it is not an either/or. It is not privacy or data use and data analytics. It is an and/and. We need to use the data, use the analytics to drive the instruction in the classroom, and hold it to the highest levels of accountability. So another example that I would give would be related to the professional learning. This goes back to the question that we were talking about a few minutes ago: How do we keep this safe? No. 1, we need to make sure we have educated teachers in the classroom, based on what can they do, what can they share, what is their responsibility.

In Quakertown, where I was, they signed a confidentiality agreement every year of what they would do and be able to share. Second, we need to take a look at our contracts. I am okay saying that, as the person that did that for the last number of years—was the contractual person. I would sit with our district solicitor and review that contract. We would not engage with a large-scale data area that was not FERPA-compliant for us. That was not highly secure with 128-byte encryption. Our student privacy and security was absolutely paramount in what we do.

We also went through State audits. Every year, I would sit with a State auditor and they would ask who has information about your data, what companies are you partnering with, what security measures do you have in place, who has access and how do you know it is safe? They would give feedback on a yearly basis. So at the State level, that leadership was also imperative.

Mr. LOEBSACK. Thank you, Mr. Murray.

Thank you, Mr. Chairman.

Mr. MEEHAN. I thank the Member.

The Chairman now recognizes the gentleman from Tennessee, Mr. Roe.

Mr. ROE. I thank the Chairman for having this hearing. Mr. Murray, I think Susan was successful because of great teachers like you. I think I would love to have my children, my three, had you in the classroom. You are very enthusiastic and bring a lot of horsepower to the classroom, I think. I think it is a tribute to you, not necessarily data. You know, we cured polio and put a man on the moon without big data. It is great teachers, I think, like you that have helped make this.

Certainly data is important. I think it is critical to find out where you are not doing well and to improve that and use it. I think the concern we have, as you can hear from all the committee Members and from the panel is, basically, privacy. I think no one right now in this country, after the NSA revelations, believes anything is private. I mean, I am here, sitting in Congress. I served on the Veterans Affairs Committee, the Education Committee. I had no idea they were doing that.

I had no earthly idea the data mining that was going on. Look, we data mine all the time. This is my Harris Teeter card. Every time I go in there they know exactly what I am buying at the Harris Teeter. So data is being mined on us all of the time. The question is, how secure and who should have it and who should care whether a kid blinks and how big they are. I mean, the concern is how is this data being used? If it is used like you are using it, it is very constructive. There is no question about it.

But the worrisome part about me is—as Mr. Reidenberg points out is that many school systems don't have the ability to contract to get these very tight and to be sure that this data is being used in a proper way. My question is: How can it be improperly used? What should we be fearful of when this data is out there in the cloud? Yes, sir.

Mr. REIDENBERG. My answer would be that the data should be used strictly for educational benefits for particular children. And begin to define, what do we mean by legitimate educational uses? That is the way I would define it. I would define it quite narrowly.

I am very concerned. I sat on a school board in my local community in New Jersey for 5 years.

Mr. ROE. My condolences.

Mr. REIDENBERG. Accepted. One of the issues that we, as a board faced, dealt with commercial—you know, advertising on the school board, in the stadium at the school. These big data programs with educational data are bringing that issue into the classroom. It is no longer just on the sports fields. I come down on the side of saying that that is not appropriate for public education. That public education, we should be using this data for the specific educational benefits of the individual children about whom the data relates. To me, that is an important public policy debate we need to have in this country.

Mr. ROE. I had no idea personally, as a parent of three children that all went to public schools, that this data was being shared with anybody. I had no idea that it would be out there for other folks to use. I think it is important that parents know that this data—I think that is absolutely critical.

Mr. REIDENBERG. Look at the case, for example—there is a bankruptcy proceeding, ConnectEDU is the company that is in bankruptcy right now. They hold data on 20 million children. One of the products that they offered was a K–12 early warning label for children. So it is not clear from the advertising. Does that mean they are labeling third-graders as not college material? They are in bankruptcy. That data can be sold off the to the highest bidder unless the trustee in bankruptcy decides to impose some restrictions on it.

The company, its main products are college counseling. So it means they are holding data on family finances because of—students were going to need student loans. The range of data they are gonna hold on those kids is quite striking.

Mr. ROE. Well, can that be used to—as Harris Teeter would do? Next thing I know, I am gonna get some coupons in the mail with what I am—is that being used to market? Is that data out there to market—whether it is loans or whatever it may be?

Mr. REIDENBERG. It is not—well, the simple answer is probably yes, but it is complicated. Because at least this particular company says that students have to designate that they want their data, say, going to a prospective college. But once the prospective college gets that information there isn't a further restriction on the college then selling it to a list broker or it bleeding out in other ways.

Mr. ROE. Yes, I think the concern you have is when you change internet service providers, you know, as I did 3 or 4 years ago. All of a sudden now—I won't mention the spam I get on here, but they obviously sold that information out and now I am getting e-mails from everybody in the world.

So I think that is a concern about how you can use it like Mr. Murray, no question it is beneficial. I think the concern is that it is not, or might not be, used like that.

Mr. REIDENBERG. We found that only 7 percent of the contracts had specific prohibitions on sale and marketing. Other contracts, and it ranged between 15 and 20 percent of the contracts, failed to restrict secondary disclosure. So some of them that restrict to secondary disclosure could encapsulate, essentially, restriction on selling it off for marketing purposes. But for explicitly, clearly saying you can't use this for marketing it is only 7 percent. You still had enormous percentages weren't even restricting any other secondary use.

Mr. ROE. Okay, Mr. Chairman, thanks for your indulgence.

Yield back.

Mr. MEEHAN. I thank the gentleman.

The Chairman now recognizes Ms. Bonamici.

Ms. BONAMICI. Thank you very much. Thank you, Chairman Meehan, Chairman Rokita, Ranking Member Clarke and Loebsack, for allowing me to participate in this fascinating discussion. This is actually an issue that comes up quite often in the district I am honored to represent out in Oregon. There have been a lot of conversations about this issue, and I really appreciate the expertise of the witnesses.

I want to follow up on the point about the opportunities. I don't think anyone would disagree that there are so many opportunities out there with technology. Mr. Murray, what you describe I have witnessed in schools in the district I represent. The use of technology to further instruction and to improve instruction, there is a lot of potential there. I don't think anyone would disagree with that. The concern is about finding the balance to make sure that that data remains adequately protected. Mr. Roe, I appreciate your sharing your little story about your Harris Teeter card.

I think the difference is that you are using that with your knowledge that they are keeping that information. You don't have to swipe that card. You were making that choice. I think that is very different for students when, often times, the parents do not understand, they do not have that same knowledge that you have about what is happening with the card that you are swiping. I have to say that whenever we are legislating around technology we have to make sure that the technology is always developing faster than policy. Policy takes a long time; technology is developing quickly.

So we have to make sure, in legislation, that we do not inhibit the positive uses but that we do the—what it takes to make the data protected. So I want to follow up. Mr. Reidenberg, you just mentioned you—the question I was gonna ask. About fewer than 7 percent of contracts between school systems and on-line service providers explicitly prohibit the sale of marketing of student information. So does that mean that the other 93 percent of contractors are selling student data? Do we have any sense of the scope of the problem?

For example, a student in my district. What are the—what is the likelihood that there is marketing going on if they are not in that 7 percent that has that prohibition?

Mr. REIDENBERG. I want to come back to the 7 percent again. The 7 percent are contracts that have specific restrictions on sale of marketing. We have other—so, for example, hosting contracts. Only 50—53 percent of the hosting contracts had any limitation on redisclosure. So that means almost half of the hosting contracts have no contractual restriction from the host service doing whatever they want with the data.

We don't have any evidence on practice, actual practices. I think that would be almost impossible to come by right now. There is

50

really not clear mechanism. I am sure we can all point to companies that will say they don't do that. I would welcome those companies presenting audit—you know, auditing, having third-party audits like they audit their financials to actually let the public know what, in fact, they are doing with school data. But there is really—other than that, there is no way to actually know systemically what the practices are in the industry.

Ms. BONAMICI. Thank you. Mr. MacCarthy, I respect the work of your organization very much. Appreciate your testimony. You did say that you do not believe that there is any new legislation required. I know that we have had this conversation about FERPA and the other existing legislation. But, Mr. Reidenberg, you said that the Department of Education has never denied Federal education funds to a school system for a violation. So I wonder, are the meaningful protections there?

Ms. Popp, thank you for talking about what Idaho is doing. But it sounds like we are gonna have to have something that has a mechanism to ensure that the school systems and the vendors are actually complying. So I want to ask Mr. MacCarthy, you state that service providers already face penalties for inappropriately disclosing information, including, for example, a 5-year ban on providing services. Has a provider ever received that penalty?

Mr. MACCARTHY. They haven't been penalized in that way. The thrust of my testimony, and maybe an opportunity to talk in more detail about this later, is that the framework set out by FERPA and that is accepted by the industry and educators throughout the country is that student information should be used solely and exclusively for educational purposes. For the benefit of the student to improve educational products and services. That is the fundamental thrust of the legal and contractual framework that exists right now in this country.

If we need to work for improving the contracts or to improve it through best practices, we are happy to step forward and to do that. But I want to reassure this committee that it is not the Wild West out there. There is not a lot of concern among educators and people directly involved in the business of educating children that a lot of information is being used for marketing purposes. I want you to pay attention to the comment that Professor Reidenberg just made. He has no evidence that this is actually happening.

His evidence is that the contracts don't prohibit it. It is against Federal law to take student information and to use it for non-educational marketing purposes——

Ms. BONAMICI. I think my—I see my time has expired. I do see we have some work to do in, perhaps, defining educational purposes. Thank you.

I yield back the balance of my time.

Mr. MURRAY. Mr. Chairman, do you mind if I say something quickly on that topic?

Mr. MEEHAN. I thank the gentlelady. No, you may finish, Mr. Murray, if you have a comment on that.

Mr. MURRAY. Sure. I would also urge caution here. Because the information that we are collecting, that we are using with third parties is very rarely comprehensive in terms of what we are transferring. I can think of three cases. Student information system,

51

medical information and, for instance, something like an on-line registration. Which are all highly encrypted. When I had signed a contract saying we will not sell and not be able to. A lot of this free stuff that are out there, most cases we are giving generic user names and passwords.

There is not actually anybody in even my district that could figure out who the child is on any of this free software or any of those free apps. Their user name might have been classroom 32, student 1. You can't do anything with that data. I do think we need to look at contracts and how important that is. But school districts are adamant that they are very careful with the information. This is not, I would agree, the Wild, Wild West in that sense that teachers and districts use very much caution in terms of anything related to student data anywhere, with the exception of the student information system where we must have it, which is highly secure, highly encrypted.

Mr. MEEHAN. Thank you. Thank you, Mr. Murray.

I am just gonna recognize myself for some closing questions. Because I promised that I would get back to Mr. MacCarthy and give him a chance to address some of this issue if he believes he didn't have an opportunity.

I am—I ask you, and appreciate that there are checks and balances on some aspects of this thing. But I am concerned, as well, as was identified when you said there is no need for future legislation. The limits, because there are places in which there are always smart people that find ways around the structure.

So when you have, perhaps, a vendor that has information, the question is where—what is it—a source of that information. What capacities do you have to rein in that vendor? Because FERPA protects your right of action against the school district, so to speak. So I look at—the question I ask is, a lot of teachers are using these perhaps outside the scope of, you know, the direction of the traditional things, or getting a lesson plan or something. The students are signing, and then that kind of private information isn't necessarily an educational record.

But the third-party vendor now owns that information. If you want to bring a right of action to say, hey, don't use it inappropriately, under FERPA the only thing we can do is punish the school district. So where is the—how do you address that issue? But I also appreciate what are the checks and balances that you are seeing that are working, that are controlling abuses of this kind of process?

Mr. MACCARTHY. So first point is that vendors, providers of services to school, are covered by FERPA. The statute that creates the school official exception reads, "A contractor is subject to the requirements of FERPA's nondisclosure rules. A contractor that violates the FERPA rules is subject to suspension of its provision of services for up to 5 years." So the legal framework is there.

Mr. MEEHAN. But didn't the Supreme Court itself say that homework assignments aren't subjected to that? Couldn't there—what is more intimate than the ability of some third party to understand the calculations that my child is making on the very math programs they are working on that third-party vendor's software?

Mr. MACCARTHY. Educators and school providers are not looking for ways to circumvent the protections of FERPA. What they are looking to do is to provide good service to students and to teachers and to schools. They treat the Personally Identifiable Information they get from schools and from students as if it deserved and should receive the fullest possible privacy protection.

Mr. MEEHAN. Mr. MacCarthy, that is a—I believe what you are saying, but that is a sweeping comment. Because we are talking about third-party vendors, and the fact is there is an awful lot of very responsible third-party vendors who completely share the same objectives. In fact, have invested in—you know, the Gates Foundation and others have invested in the best ways to teach. We don't want to stifle that. But we also know that there are third-party vendors out there who are looking at finding consumer information, any access they can get to something that helps them.

So what is the protection against when my child is swiping his card to see what he eats to make sure that he doesn't get free— you know, free things from Coca-Cola?

Mr. MACCARTHY. On that particular point, FERPA recently issued some guidance. They said explicitly that a service provider such as a cafeteria provider or an e-mail provider is prohibited by Federal law from providing targeted advertising to the students based on the information it collects as part of its school service. It is currently illegal to do that, and the Department of Education just released that advice in February of this year.

Mr. MEEHAN. Mr. Reidenberg, do you have any comment with regard to whether there are other—to that information, or whether there are other gaps in the system?

Mr. REIDENBERG. Yes. I think—I mean, a whole host. To that specific point, it is guidance, it is not regulation. The Department did not go through an administrative procedure act regulatory process. It is wrong on the law. I think that the gaps are astounding. Twenty-five percent of the—these kinds of services are offered at a premium to the school; 25 percent of the contracts we saw. That means they are monetizing the data somehow. That monetization is not going to be coming from educational benefits targeted to particular children.

We have seen this with Google apps for education. They represented they weren't data mining e-mail, student e-mail. Turns out they were. That came out in a lawsuit. I think right now we are at a point where we need to modernize FERPA and we need to modernize it. There are a series of steps that have to take place for—has to apply to all student information. It has to mandate notice to parents, public disclosure, of these arrangements that just don't exist right now. What the educational uses are.

I can give you further points, I think. That school districts have to have written contracts with specific prohibitions. I disagree quite strongly with the statement Mr. MacCarthy just made about the applicability of FERPA to vendors. I don't think that is what the statute says. If he and I can each disagree on something like that, I think that may suggest it is time for Congress to take a look at what the statute means. States need to have chief privacy officers. There are a lot of districts out there that don't have the resources to address these issue and these problems.

53

They need guidance, they need it desperately. There need to be remedies. Right now, there are no remedies. We have a long tradition in this country that we sort out some of these problems through private actions. Well, today we have no mechanism for that. If any of the—if an irresponsible vendor out there does something grossly inappropriate with student information there is no remedy. The parents, the families, they have no remedy whatsoever——

Mr. MEEHAN. Okay. Well, I thank you, Mr. Reidenberg.

I just wanted to ask one thing. Ms. Popp, you have worked very diligently as a system, a State system, to look at the square of this issue and try to—have you built in protections against the kinds of things Mr. Reidenberg is pointing out, or are those gaps still there?

Ms. POPP. From Idaho's perspective, I believe we have worked very diligently to build in the safeguards. I think awareness is absolutely the key, and training and working with the school districts, to Mr. Reidenberg's point. In Idaho, we have many rural and remote districts. They may not have the resources. I think this is one time that the State can step in at a State level and help them understand what they need to have in place and the safeguards. All school districts within the State of Idaho have school boards, and those school boards do have representation from their own legal counsel for the most part.

There may be one or two that does not. However, again, doing the diligent training on what a good contract looks like, helping them understand the protections of the data and, to Mr. Murray's point, putting in the technology protections of the encryption any time data is transferred is key to making this work.

Mr. MEEHAN. Well, I thank you. I think one panelist has one more question.

Mr. Rokita.

Mr. ROKITA. Thank you. This will be pretty quick. In fact, let the record reflect that of my 5 minutes, 3 has been used already. So with that, let me just again thank the witnesses. Appreciate even more Idaho's approach. State by State, this is still, I think, the way to go for this. Lacking a Constitutional basis otherwise. There may be one, but that is for another hearing on another day.

We have talked about FERPA a lot. But you, Mr. MacCarthy, mentioned some other pieces of legislation, some acts. The Children's Online Privacy Protection Act, correct? You said that requires parents' permission before the use of data. But you also said that it only applies to children up to the age of 13. Can you reconcile the two, or what?

Mr. MACCARTHY. You stated it accurately. It is designed to protect children in the on-line context.

Mr. ROKITA. So after 14.

Mr. MACCARTHY. After 14 it does not apply.

Mr. ROKITA. After 13. Okay, I just wanted to clear that up. So it is not a—it is not a total solution either, is it?

Mr. MACCARTHY. It protects children. Its aim is to protect children. Teenagers are out from under its coverage. The remaining protections of FERPA, the FERPA protection, contractual protection is the best practices. Those still stay in place. COPPA's aimed at children 13 and under.

Mr. ROKITA. Okay, thank you. While it is acknowledged, and certainly came out in the testimony today, that FERPA does not recognize a private right of action, there still is a common law contractual breach right of action. Yes or no, Mr. Reidenberg?

Mr. REIDENBERG. Only with respect to the school district. If the provision is in the contract between the district and the vendor, the district would be able to enforce the contract. The victim child and family, at best, would be a third-party beneficiary and would very likely have great difficulty bringing any sort of action. Again, that is assuming the contract includes a protection—an underlying protection in the first place.

Mr. ROKITA [continuing]. Which goes to my earlier question. It may be a legal malpractice case, but that is a stretch, too.

Mr. MACCARTHY. Mr. Chairman, just to be clear. One of the reasons to work with Joel and with other people to make sure that the contracts contain the appropriate provisions is precisely to create this extra enforcement mechanism. We are all looking forward to that.

Mr. ROKITA. But you are not for private right of action.

Mr. MACCARTHY. I don't think a private right of action would be appropriate. But I do think the ability for the schools to go into court and enforce against vendors who do the wrong thing using contractual violations would be a good thing.

Mr. ROKITA. How would you measure damages?

Mr. MACCARTHY. I don't have a good answer for that.

Mr. ROKITA. See, that is a problem, too. Unless you have some statutory damages built in, like Idaho did, right? Which you support.

Mr. MACCARTHY. That would be a step in the right direction at the State level.

Mr. ROKITA. You being Mr. MacCarthy for the purposes of the record. Ten more seconds.

Mr. REIDENBERG. Mr. Chairman, I was just going to say for a school district to enforce a contract, as a former school board member if I am facing an instance where there is some sort of breach that takes place, and I have to decide to devote $50,000 to $100,000 of taxpayer money to litigate that, that is gonna be a hard decision for local school boards to be making. So again, if it is total reliance on the school board protecting their children's privacy it may be a very difficult thing to do where the harm is particularized to just a couple families.

Mr. ROKITA. Mr. Chairman, thank you again for your leadership with this hearing.

I yield back.

Mr. MURRAY. Mr. Chairman, can I respectfully—one more—one last comment?

Mr. MEEHAN. Go ahead, Mr. Murray.

Mr. MURRAY. I heard today a lot about vendors. I have heard today a lot about third parties. Privacy is absolutely real. My encouragement is to hold the expectation high for all of them to build in safeguards at the State level, like Ms. Popp eloquently shared. School districts need to be transparent, and transparent with their families in what they are collecting and what they are doing with that data. But what we cannot have happen is that we cannot stifle the incredible innovation that is going on with personalized learning and the awesome teachers we have in our Nation.

Thank you.

Mr. MEEHAN. Well, thank you, Mr. Murray. You got the last word, and a good one it was. But I think the last word on what was a very invigorating presentation by the panel.

I want to thank my colleagues for their very genuine interest in this particular issue. I want to thank you, the panelists, who I know are continuing to work out there in the field for your work. We will monitor your continuing work. I thank you for the efforts that you all put, as well, into the education of our next generation of children.

The Members of the committee may have some additional questions for the witnesses. If, in fact, they do go we would ask that you would do your best to be responsive in writing. I thank you again for all of your testimony. Without objection, the subcommittee stands adjourned.

[Whereupon, at 12:41 p.m., the subcommittees were adjourned.]

○

www.ingramcontent.com/pod-product-compliance
Lightning Source LLC
Chambersburg PA
CBHW060441060326
40690CB00019B/4289